Workbook to Accompany

Understanding Medical Coding:

A Comprehensive Guide

SECOND EDITION

Prepared by Sandra L. Johnson
Lecturer of Biology/Allied Health
Indiana University Southeast

DELMAR
CENGAGE Learning

Australia • Brazil • Japan • Korea • Mexico • Singapore • Spain • United Kingdom • United States

DELMAR
CENGAGE Learning

Workbook to Accompany Understanding Medical Coding: A Comprehensive Guide, Second Edition
Sandra L. Johnson

Vice President, Health Care Business Unit: William Brottmiller

Editorial Director: Matthew Kane

Acquisitions Editor: Rhonda Dearborn

Developmental Editor: Sarah Duncan

Editorial Assistant: Debra S. Gorgos

Marketing Director: Jennifer McAvey

Marketing Coordinator: Kimberly Duffy

Technology Director: Laurie K. Davis

Technology Project Manager: Mary Colleen Liburdi

Production Director: Carolyn Miller

Senior Production Editor: James Zayicek

Library of Congress Control Number: 2006003055

ISBN-13: 978-1-4180-1045-4

ISBN-10: 1-4180-1045-6

Delmar
Executive Woods
5 Maxwell Drive
Clifton Park, NY 12065
USA

Cengage Learning is a leading provider of customized learning solutions with office locations around the globe, including Singapore, the United Kingdom, Australia, Mexico, Brazil, and Japan. Locate your local office at **www.cengage.com/global**

Cengage Learning products are represented in Canada by Nelson Education, Ltd.

To learn more about Delmar, visit **www.cengage.com/delmar**

Purchase any of our products at your local bookstore or at our preferred online store **www.CengageBrain.com**

Notice to the Reader
Publisher does not warrant or guarantee any of the products described herein or perform any independent analysis in connection with any of the product information contained herein. Publisher does not assume, and expressly disclaims, any obligation to obtain and include information other than that provided to it by the manufacturer. The reader is expressly warned to consider and adopt all safety precautions that might be indicated by the activities described herein and to avoid all potential hazards. By following the instructions contained herein, the reader willingly assumes all risks in connection with such instructions. The publisher makes no representations or warranties of any kind, including but not limited to, the warranties of fitness for particular purpose or merchantability, nor are any such representations implied with respect to the material set forth herein, and the publisher takes no responsibility with respect to such material. The publisher shall not be liable for any special, consequential, or exemplary damages resulting, in whole or part, from the readers' use of, or reliance upon, this material.

Printed in the United States of America
6 7 8 9 10   14 13 12 11 10
ED312

Contents

Chapter 1
Introduction to Coding

The *Occupational Outlook Handbook* published by the U.S. Department of Labor–Bureau of Labor Statistics, predicts an increasing demand for occupations related to the field of health information management. This includes coders, insurance specialists, and billing and reimbursement specialists. Career opportunities include medical practices, hospitals, insurance companies, government agencies, and private coding and billing services. Those with experience in these areas can also work as consultants, educators, auditors, and trainers.

Training requirements include anatomy and physiology, medical terminology, coding, critical thinking, and computer and data entry skills. Once training is accomplished, certification and membership in one or more professional associations, and maintaining a professional credential is not only recommended, but often required. Some of these associations are the American Academy of Professional Coders (AAPC), American Health Information Management Association (AHIMA), and the Board of Advanced Medical Coding (BAMC). The National Electronic Billers Alliance (NEBA) and the American Medical Billing Association (AMBA) are associations providing credentials to claim and reimbursement specialists.

REVIEW QUESTIONS

Visit the AAPC web site at www.aapc.com and answer the following questions.

1. List the three methods of certification offered by the American Academy of Professional Coders (AAPC).

   a.

   b.

   c.

2. List five examples of how to obtain preapproved CEUs offered by the AAPC.

   a.

   b.

   c.

   d.

   e.

3. AAPC now offers specialty credentials. Identify three of these and compare areas covered in each specialty exam.

4. Visit the American Hospital Information Management Association (AHIMA) web site at www.ahima.org. Compare the coding CCS and CCS-P credentials of AHIMA with the CPC and CPC-H of AAPC.

5. Advanced coding certification is available through the Board of Advanced Medical Coding (BAMC). Visit their web site at www.advancedmedicalcoding.com for information on Advanced Coding Specialist (ACS) credentials available in a variety of specialties. What is the purpose or advantage of seeking an ACS credential?

Fraud and Abuse

Chapter 1 defines fraud and abuse as defined by the Health Insurance Portability and Accountability Act (HIPAA) of 1996.

REVIEW QUESTIONS

Identify the activities below as "abuse" (A) or "fraud" (F).

F 1. A simple wound repair of a laceration to the forehead is coded complex in order to receive higher reimbursement.

F 2. The date for symptoms related to a preexisting condition is changed so the patient may qualify for insurance benefits.

A 3. A primary care physician refers all female patients to a gynecologist for routine pelvic/breast exam and Pap smear.

F 4. The laboratory components of a comprehensive metabolic panel are coded and billed individually instead of using the panel code.

F 5. A physician refers patients to a particular pharmacy in order to receive a discount on medications ordered and used in the office.

F 6. An internationally known manufacturer recognized for its cardiac products offers a cardiovascular surgeon and the clinic staff an all-expense-paid trip to Aruba for the exclusive use of its products.

A 7. Refunds are not issued for services determined not reasonable and necessary by Medicare.

F 8. An uninsured patient seen in the Emergency Department "borrows" a friend's insurance card to receive medical care.

A 9. A medical office bills for telephone calls for prescription refills without advanced notification to the patient.

A 10. A medical practice finds it is easier to routinely bill the patient for co-payment instead of collecting it at time of service.

Medical Terminology

An essential training element in medical coding is medical terminology. ICD-9-CM, CPT, and HCPCS code books utilize medical terms and a medical coder must be knowledgeable in the language of medicine and its usage as well as the anatomy of the human body.

REVIEW QUESTIONS

Select the correct term for the following.

1. What is the medical term for an obstetrical or vaginal repair?
   a. Colpectomy
   b. Episiotomy
   c. Vaginectomy
   d. Vaginorrhaphy

2. What is cholecystitis with cholelithiasis?
   a. Inflammation of the gallbladder with gallstones
   b. Inflammation of the stomach and lower intestinal tract
   c. Ulceration of the colon
   d. Internal and external hemorrhoids

3. What is the medical term for removal of the eye?
   a. Enucleation = total removal of
   b. Evacuation
   c. Ophthalmoscopy
   d. Orbitectomy

4. What is the medical term for removal of fluid from the knee joint?
   a. Arthrocentesis
   b. Arthrodesis
   c. Arthoplasty
   d. Arthroscopy

5. What is an ileus?
   a. Inflammation of the hip bone
   b. Intestinal inflammation
   c. Intestinal obstruction
   d. Skin disorder

6. What does gastrodynia mean?
   a. Abdominal fissure
   b. Abdominal pain
   c. Intestinal virus
   d. Rectal spasm

7. In the diagnosis "carcinoma of the liver metastatic to the pancreas," what does metastatic mean?
   a. The cancer has spread to the liver.
   b. The cancer has spread to the pancreas.
   c. The cancer is in remission.
   d. The cancer is in terminal stages.

8. What is the meaning of glossopharyngeal?
   a. Pertaining to the mouth and throat
   b. Pertaining to the tongue and throat
   c. Pertaining to the esophagus and throat
   d. Pertaining to the glands and throat

9. The term keratin refers to what anatomical system?
   a. Endocrinology
   b. Female reproductive
   c. Integumentary
   d. Musculoskeletal

10. What does the term gravida mean?
   a. A benign lesion
   b. A pregnant woman
   c. The weight of a substance
   d. Transplanting skin or tissue

11. What is the term used to mean a specimen is visible to the naked eye?
   a. Gross
   b. Insulate
   c. Isolate
   d. Microscopic

12. What is onychocryptosis?
   a. Excessive granulation tissue
   b. Inflamed hair follicle
   c. Infection of an ingrown nail
   d. Skin rash

13. What is hematemesis?
   a. Blood in urine
   b. Coughing up blood
   c. Rectal bleeding
   d. Vomiting of blood

14. What is melena?
   a. Blood in sputum
   b. Blood in stools
   c. Blood in urine
   d. Blood in nasal drainage

15. What is the medical term for painful menstruation?
   a. Amenorrhea
   b. Dysplasia
   c. Dysmenorrhea
   d. Menometrorrhagia

Medical Necessity

Documentation in a medical record must be complete, legible, and accurate to appropriately assign Evaluation and Management codes and link them to the correct ICD-9-CM codes to provide medical necessity for the service or procedure provided.

REVIEW QUESTIONS

In the following list of terms, link the correct diagnosis to the appropriate service or procedure to show medical necessity to the insurance company.

Diagnosis		Procedure/Service	
d	1. Chest pain	A.	Urinalysis
h	2. Neoplasm of breast	B.	Lavage to remove earwax
f	3. Type II diabetes	C.	Fracture
i	4. Pneumonia	D.	Electrocardiogram
g	5. Sore throat	E.	Lipid panel
j	6. Severe prolapse of eyelids	F.	Fasting glucose
c	7. Closed reduction of femur	G.	Strep test
a	8. Dysuria and pyuria	H.	Mastectomy
e	9. Hypercholesterolemia	I.	Chest x-ray
b	10. Impacted cerumen	J.	Blepharoplasty

Chapter 2
ICD-9-CM

ICD-9-CM contains codes for diagnoses, symptoms, illnesses, and diseases. Volume 1 contains the tabular numerical listing of diagnosis codes. Volume 2 contains the alphabetic listing of diagnoses. Volumes 1 and 2 are used by all health care facilities for coding the reason for the patient's encounter whether in the physician's office, hospital, nursing facility, or in-home care. Volume 3 contains a tabular and alphabetic listing of procedures primarily used in the hospital inpatient setting. (Coding exercises for Volume 3 are included in Chapter 16 of this workbook.)

Volume 1, the Classification of Diseases and Injuries, contains 17 chapters grouped according to the cause or body system, such as neoplasms. V codes, E codes, and M codes are also included in Volume 1.

Since Volume 2 contains the alphabetic index, the coder must look here first to locate the code for the diagnosis or reason the patient has presented for a medical encounter. The code is then verified in the numerical list of Volume 1. It is important to always cross-check the term in Volume 1 with the description of the term in Volume 2 in order to verify the code and to check the fifth-digit requirement. Chapter 2 of the textbook describes the steps to follow in locating the main term, identifying subterms, and verifying the code in the tabular list.

V codes can be used to describe the reason for the patient's visit when the patient is not sick or does not have a medical complaint. Many of these codes are used to code routine services, a family or personal history of a condition, and screening or testing when a patient is exposed to a disease or illness.

E codes are external causes of injury that are used as secondary codes to show the reason of an injury, such as an automobile accident or a fall. E codes are also used to report poisonings, toxic effects of substances, or drug overdoses.

M codes are morphology codes and are used primarily by cancer registries to identify the cell type and behavior of a neoplasm in conjunction with the neoplasm code from the neoplasm table. M codes are not used for insurance reimbursement reporting purposes.

Coding Exercises

Code the following exercises using Volumes 1 and 2 of ICD-9-CM.

1. Mass in breast — 611.72

2. Shadow on lung seen on chest x-ray, etiology undetermined — 793.1

3. History of allergy to penicillin — V14.0

4. Carcinoma of sigmoid colon *primary* metastatic to peritoneum — 153.3 197.6

5. Migraine headache — 346.90

6. Internal and external thrombosed hemorrhoids — 455.4 455.1

7. NIDDM with diabetic skin ulcer — ~~249.8~~ 707.9
   250.80

8. Carbuncle of eyelid   373.13

9. Chest pain, probable angina pectoris   786.50

10. Positive tuberculin test   795.5

11. Benign growth of labia majora   221.2

12. Diabetic gangrene   25070   785.4

13. Carcinoma in situ of the cervix uteri   233.1

14. Amenorrhea   626.0

15. Benign hypertrophy of prostate   600.00

AAPC Certification Questions

1. Which one of the following is an example of an eponym?
   a. Alzheimer's disease
   b. Epistaxis
   c. Seborrheic dermatitis
   d. Syncope

2. A malignant neoplasm is removed from the lower-outer quadrant of the right breast. There is metastasis to the right lung. What are the correct codes?
   a. 174.5; 162.9
   b. 174.5; 197.0
   c. 174.9; 197.0
   d. 239.3; 239.1

3. A laboratory report indicated an abnormal result on a patient's Mantoux test required for his employment in a nursing facility. What is the correct code?
   a. 010.90
   b. 795.5
   c. 795.79
   d. V74.1

4. A 49-year-old patient is in the office complaining of severe chest pain. An acute MI is suspected but a conclusive diagnosis is pending additional studies to be done at the hospital. Until a definite diagnosis has been determined, how would this be coded in the office for the physician's bill?
   a. 410.90
   b. 786.5
   c. 786.50
   d. 786.59

5. A patient is brought into the Emergency Department for syncope and hypotension. After examination and testing, no medical reason could be determined for the symptoms. What are the correct codes?
   a. 780.09; 458.9
   b. 780.2; 401.9
   c. 780.2; 458.9
   d. 780.4; 458.9

6. An AIDS patient is seen in the office with skin lesions over his back which are suspicious for Kaposi's sarcoma. An incisional biopsy confirms this diagnosis. What are the correct codes?

    a. 042; 176.0

    b. 042; 176.9

    c. 042; 709.9

    d. 042; 709.9; 176.0

7. A patient is in the office complaining of involuntary movement of her legs with an itchy feeling, especially at night when she goes to bed. The diagnosis today is restless leg syndrome. What is the correct code?

    a. 333.90

    b. 333.99

    c. 781.0

    d. 799.2

8. A patient with Type I diabetes mellitus seriously out of control is admitted for regulation of insulin dosage. He also complains of some chest discomfort. The patient had been in the hospital four weeks earlier for an acute myocardial infarction of the inferoposterior wall, and an EKG was performed to check the patient's current cardiac status. What are the correct codes for the most recent visit?

    a. 250.00; 410.32

    b. 250.03; 410.32

    c. 250.03; 410.30

    d. 250.80; 410.32

9. A patient is scheduled for outpatient testing for complaints of urinary retention and enlargement of the prostate. He returns to the office for follow-up and the results after the tests are completed. The diagnosis is adenocarcinoma of the prostate with metastasis to the bone. What are the correct codes?

    a. 185; 198.5

    b. 185; 198.5; M8010/6

    c. 239.5; 170.9

    d. 239.5; 170.9; M8010/6

10. A housekeeper cleaning a room in the hospital is exposed to blood-tainted emesis. What is the correct code?

    a. 578.0

    b. 994.9

    c. V01.9

    d. V15.85

REVIEW QUESTIONS

1. Explain the steps used to code a patient's complaint of diarrhea.

2. Explain the difference between a principal diagnosis and a primary diagnosis.

3. NOS is an abbreviation used in ICD-9-CM to indicate unspecified when the _____ has no further information to fully define or describe the condition.

4. NEC is an abbreviation used in ICD-9-CM to indicate a more specific category is not available in _____.

5. Indicate which of the following is identified as a V code by placing an "x" in the space provided.

_____ a. Nausea, vomiting, abdominal pain

_____ b. Exposure to patient with tuberculosis

_____ c. Annual gynecological exam with Pap smear

_____ d. Elevated blood pressure reading

_____ e. Flu vaccination

_____ f. Abnormal electrocardiogram

_____ g. Encounter for contraceptive counseling and management

_____ h. Family history of breast carcinoma

_____ i. Normal pregnancy

_____ j. Screening for hyperthyroidism

Chapter 3
Health Care Common Procedure Coding System (HCPCS)

The Healthcare Common Procedure Coding System (HCPCS) is a three-level coding system. HCPCS Level I is AMA/CPT. HCPCS Level II, maintained by the Centers for Medicare and Medicaid Services (CMS), contains national codes used to identify procedures, supplies, medications (with the exception of vaccines), equipment, and items. Vaccines and immunizations are assigned CPT codes. HCPCS Level III contained CMS local codes until its deletion in December 2003 under the HIPAA rule. Many of these codes were moved to HCPCSII.

There are 22 sections of HCPCSII as follows:

Transportation Services	A0000–A0999
Medical and Surgical Supplies	A4000–A8999
Miscellaneous and Experimental	A9000–A9999
Enteral and Parenteral Therapy	B4000–B9999
Temporary Hospital Outpatient PPS	C1000–C9999
Dental Procedures	D0000–D9999
Durable Medical Equipment (DME)	E0100–E9999
Temporary Procedures and Services	G0000–G9999
Rehabilitative Services	H0001–H1005
Drugs Administered Other than Oral Method	J0000–J8999
Chemotherapy Drugs	J9000–J9999
Temporary Codes for DMERCS (Durable Medical Equipment Regional Carriers)	K0000–K9999
Orthotic Procedures	L0100–L4999
Prosthetic Procedures	L5000–L5600
Medical Services	M0000–M0399
Pathology and Laboratory	P0000–P2999
Temporary Codes	Q0000–Q9999
Diagnostic Radiology Services	R0000–R5999
Temporary National Codes	S0000–S9999
State Medicaid Agency Codes	T1000–T9999
Vision Services	V0000–V2999
Hearing Services	V5000–V5299

When assigning codes for drugs, both generic and trade names are listed, although codes are assigned to the generic names. The brand or trade names are referred to the proper generic name. Close attention must be paid to the amount column that refers to amount of drug dispensed in order to assign the correct code. It is also important to know the various routes of administration of a drug:

IA	Intra-arterial	INH	Inhalation
IV	Intravenous	INJ	Injection not otherwise specified
IM	Intramuscular	VAR	Various routes
IT	Intrathecal	OTH	Other routes
SC	Subcutaneous	ORAL	Administered orally

Coding Exercises

Assign HCPCSII codes to the following.

1. Inhalation of nasal vaccine   J3530

2. Morphine 10 mg. IV   J2270

3. Evaluation for hearing aid   V5010

4. Adjustable aluminum quad prong cane   E0105

5. Alcohol wipes, per box   A4245

6. Emergency ambulance service, advanced life support   A0427

7. Vitamin B12 800 mcg. IM   J3420

8. Silicone breast prosthesis   L8030

9. Mobile commode chair with detachable arms   E0165

10. Standard wheelchair, fixed arms and foot rests   E1130   T1013

11. Sign language interpreter, 30 minutes   G0153×2   T08 × 2

12. Mitomycin 25 mg. for chemotherapy   J9280   ×5

13. Two units red blood cells for transfusion   P9021×2

14. Portable ECG transported to nursing facility, one patient   R0076

15. Routine transportation of patient in wheelchair van   A0130

AAPC Certification Review

1. Valium 5 mg. is ordered by the physician to be administered to a patient IM. HCPCSII lists the code by generic name. What is the generic name for Valium?
   a. Diazepam
   b. Furosemide
   c. Haloperidol
   d. Lorazepam

2. An 18-year-old female comes into the OB/GYN clinic for an injection of Depo-Provera 150 mg. for contraceptive purposes. What is the correct code?

 a. J1000

 b. J1051 x 3

 c. J1055

 d. J1056

3. A 55-year-old female, diagnosed with breast cancer, undergoes a unilateral simple mastectomy with implantation of a silicone prosthesis. What is the correct code?

 a. L8020

 b. L8030

 c. L8600

 d. L8699

4. A patient is given injectable Bicillin L-A 1,200,000 units IM for strep throat. What is the correct code?

 a. J0530 x 2

 b. J0540   J0561 x2

 c. J0560 x 2

 d. J0570

5. A patient is critically injured in a motorcycle accident. When emergency medical technicians arrive, preparation is made to stat-flight the patient by helicopter to a trauma center in a nearby city. What is the correct code?

 a. A0422

 b. A0427

 c. A0430

 d. A0431

6. A Medicare patient has a skin tag removed in the physician's office. A surgical tray is used for this minor procedure. The specimen is sent to pathology for testing. What is the code for the surgical tray?

 a. 11200

 b. 88304

 c. 99070

 d. A4550

7. Which one of the following is an example of an inhalation drug?

 a. Albuterol

 b. Amitriptyline

 c. Estradiol valerate

 d. Phenobarbital

8. What category of HCPCSII codes is developed and recognized by commercial payers, such as BlueCross/BlueShield?

 a. A codes

 b. C codes

 c. S codes

 d. T codes

9. A hospital bed with electric head, foot, and height adjustments, including mattress and side rails is rented for home use. What is the correct code?
   a. E0250-RR
   b. E0255-RR
   c. E0260-RR
   d. E0265-RR

10. A 52-year-old male with Type II diabetes is fitted for a custom-prepared and molded shoe from a cast of the patient's foot. What is the correct code?
    a. A5500
    b. A5501
    c. A5507
    d. A5511

REVIEW QUESTIONS

1. Match the route of medication administration with the correct term.

   _C_ Intrathecal   a. Within the muscle
   _d_ Intravenous   b. p.o. (by mouth)
   _e_ Subcutaneous   c. Within a sheath
   _f_ Inhalation   d. Within a vein
   _a_ Intramuscular   e. Beneath the layers of the skin
   _b_ Oral   f. Breathing in

2. In what section of HCPCSII would you locate the code for a CPAP device? *Continuous positive airway pressure*
   a. Durable medical equipment
   b. Medical and surgical supplies
   c. Orthotic procedures
   d. Rehabilitative services

3. Which one of the following is a DME?
   a. Blood glucose monitor
   b. Dentures
   c. Ostomy supplies
   d. Vascular catheters

4. What CPT code is used for all supplies, medications, and equipment not applicable to HCPCSII? What must be attached with the claim to obtain reimbursement?

   99070 tray, supplies, materials
   _____

5. Which one of the following is an example of a diagnostic radiology service?
   a. Enteral nutrition infusion pump
   b. Portable x-ray equipment with personnel to nursing facility
   c. Screening Pap smear
   d. Venipuncture for collection of specimen

Chapter 4
Current Procedural Terminology (CPT) Coding Basics

Current procedural terminology (CPT) is a five-digit numerical code used to describe specific medical services and procedures performed by physicians and other health care providers. First introduced in 1966, the current edition is referred to as CPT-4.

Knowledge of medical terminology is necessary to assign codes to services and procedures to a third-party payer and to link ICD-9-CM codes to prove medical necessity.

CPT is divided into six sections: Evaluation and Management, Anesthesia, Surgery, Radiology, Pathology and Laboratory, and Medicine. A listing of Category II and III codes, Appendices A–I, and the Index are included. Modifiers are two-digit numbers added to the basic CPT code to indicate special circumstances in the description of the CPT code.

Coding Exercises

Assign codes to the following using all chapters of CPT. Assign modifier as indicated.

1. Puncture aspiration of cyst of breast   19000
2. I & D of thyroid gland cyst   60000
3. Complete x-ray of the scapula   73010
4. I & D hematoma of right wrist   25028 / R
5. Blood pressure check by nurse   99211
6. Laryngoscopy endoscopy, indirect   31505
7. Neuroplasty for carpal tunnel syndrome, bilateral   64721 - 50
8. Complete radiologic exam of the mandible   70110
9. Incisional biopsy of testis   54505
10. Intradermal test for tuberculosis   86580
11. Medical testimony as subpoenaed by insurance company   99075-32
12. Tonsillectomy and adenoidectomy, age 15, assistant surgeon   42821 - 80
13. Office visit, EPF, patient last seen 5 years ago   99202
14. Flexible colonoscopy with biopsy   45380

AAPC Certification Review

Select the proper CPT codes.

1. A new patient is seen in the office for a needle biopsy of the testis for suspected testicular carcinoma.
   a. 99202, 54500
   b. 99202, 54505
   c. 99212, 54500
   d. 99212, 10021

2. The patient later undergoes a simple bilateral orchiectomy.
   a. 54520-50
   b. 54522-50
   c. 54530-50
   d. 54690-50

3. A 16-year-old male is seen in the emergency room for a laceration of the scalp measuring 3.5 cm. A problem-focused exam is performed and an intermediate repair of the laceration is made.
   a. 99281, 12002
   b. 99281, 12013
   c. 99281, 12032
   d. 99281, 12052

4. A new patient is evaluated in the urgent care center for an injury to the left leg. An x-ray is taken of the tibia and fibula (two views), which confirms a fracture. The patient is referred to an orthopedic surgeon for treatment.
   a. 99202, 73590-LT
   b. 99212, 73590-LT
   c. 99241, 73590-LT
   d. 99281, 73590-LT

5. A patient is referred to the hospital laboratory for an electrolyte panel, automated CBC with automated differential WBC, and a nonautomated urinalysis with microscopy.
   a. 80051, 85004, 81000
   b. 80051, 85025, 81000
   c. 80051, 85025, 81001
   d. 80051, 85027, 81000

6. A new patient is seen in the office for infection of the left great toenail. The patient also has Type II diabetes mellitus. An expanded problem-focused office visit is performed as well as an incision and drainage of the abscess of the left great toenail. A sterile tray is used for the simple procedure.
   a. 99202, 10060, 99070
   b. 99212, 10060, 99070
   c. 99202, 10061, 99070
   d. 99202, 10160, 99070

7. Referring to the case in question 6, this patient returns for recheck of the infected area three days later. The area has healed well with no additional treatment today. He does have blood drawn for a glucose to be sent to the laboratory.
   a. 99202, 36415
   b. 99212, 36415
   c. 99212, 36415, 82947
   d. 99212, 82947

8. An established patient is admitted to the hospital on Monday, followed in the hospital on Tuesday, with discharge on Wednesday. Hospital admission and subsequent visit are all straightforward medical decision making. The planning and management to discharge the patient takes 25 minutes.
   a. 99218, 99217
   b. 99221, 99231, 99238
   c. 99221, 99231, 99239
   d. 99234, 99238

9. Dr. Smith assists Dr. Brown with a craniotomy for drainage of an intracranial abscess.
   a. 61320
   b. 61320-80
   c. 61546-80
   d. 61570-80

10. A 45-year-old patient is seen as a new patient to the practice for a comprehensive physical examination. He has no complaints. He will return as needed (prn).
    a. 99204
    b. 99205
    c. 99244
    d. 99386

REVIEW QUESTIONS

1. List the six sections of CPT.

   _____

   _____

   _____

   _____

   _____

   _____

2. What edition is the current publication of CPT? _____

3. What does the + symbol indicate in CPT?
   a. Add-on code
   b. Modifier
   c. Multiple codes
   d. New code

4. Where can a list of all modifiers be located in CPT?
   a. Appendix A
   b. Appendix B
   c. Appendix C
   d. Appendix D

5. Match the following modifiers with their usage.

   _____ Prolonged E/M service   a. -54
   _____ Anesthesia by surgeon   b. -90
   _____ Assistant surgeon   c. -54
   _____ Bilateral procedure   d. -21
   _____ Reduced services   e. -91
   _____ Professional component   f. -47
   _____ Surgical care only   g. -52
   _____ Discontinued procedure   h. -50
   _____ Reference laboratory   i. -26
   _____ Repeat laboratory test   j. -80

Chapter 5
Evaluation and Management

The first section of CPT introduces Evaluation and Management (E/M) codes. These codes are used for provider services based on the examination of the patient in various settings, such as office, hospital, emergency room, or nursing facility.

Documentation in the medical record is a key factor in selecting an appropriate CPT code, as well as the ICD-9-CM code. Questions such as who, what, when, where, and why are essential to assigning codes. *REMEMBER: If it is not documented, it did not happen!*

Coding Exercises

Assign E/M codes to the following.

1. Detailed consultation, new patient (pt.), inpatient — *99253*

2. Well-child checkup, established (est.) pt., age 7 — *99393*

3. Office consultation, new pt., second opinion for tonsillectomy/adenoidectomy — *99241*

99241
99245

4. Office visit, est. pt., expanded problem focused (EPF) history (hx.)/exam, LC — *99213*

5. Admission to hospital, initial hospital care, straightforward, detailed history and exam — *99221*

6. Subsequent hospital care, medical decision of moderate complexity, expanded problem — *99232*

7. Hospital discharge, 30 minutes to discuss medications — *99238*

8. Emergency department care, minimal care, PF, straightforward — *99281*

9. Initial inpatient consultation, new pt., moderate complexity, comprehensive history and exam — *99254*

10. Initial office consultation, medical decision of high complexity, second opinion for surgical opinion. — *99245*

11. Rest home visit, evaluation of new pt., moderate complexity, EPF — *99325*

12. Admission to skilled nursing facility, est. pt., detailed history, comprehensive exam — *99304*

13. Patient admitted to post-op observation bed following laparoscopic cholecystectomy at 10 a.m. with discharge 5 p.m. same day — *99235*

14. New pt. examined and treated in urgent care center, EPF <u>99202</u>

15. Pediatric critical care, initial, inpatient, age 9 months <u>99471</u>

AAPC Certification Review

1. An established patient was seen by the CMA to have his blood pressure checked. B/P today is 140/90, which is lower from last B/P check one week ago. He will return in one week for recheck. Select the proper code.
   a. 99211
   b. 99212
   c. 99261
   d. 99271

2. A patient was seen by her family physician with a recommendation to have a hysterectomy. The patient consulted another physician for a second opinion. This visit is coded
   a. an established patient office visit
   b. a follow-up consultation
   c. an expanded problem-focused office visit for a new patient
   d. an initial office consultation

3. What is the correct modifier to use when a consultation is required by a third party?
   a. -22
   b. -32
   c. -54
   d. -57

4. An 87-year-old female was admitted to the nursing home after discharge from the hospital for management and physical therapy for a fracture of the left femur. Her primary care physician came by the facility to discharge the patient to home care, spending 20 minutes with the patient and her family. This is coded
   a. 99217
   b. 99238
   c. 99315
   d. 99321

5. A physician in the emergency department (ED) of a hospital examines an 18-year-old with the complaint of recurrent, severe menstrual migraine headache. Medications administered in the ED significantly relieves the patient's symptoms. This is coded
   a. 99241
   b. 99281
   c. 99282
   d. 99284

6. A physician performs an independent medical examination to determine and rate impairment for disability for Workers' Compensation benefits. This is coded
   a. 99450
   b. 99455
   c. 99456
   d. 99420

7. A patient is seen for follow-up in the office for post-op mastectomy with an expanded problem-focused visit and examination for diabetes, newly detected and treated. This is coded
   a. 99202
   b. 99214
   c. 99214-24
   d. 99214-58

8. A patient is admitted to the observation area of the hospital to monitor elevated blood pressure readings following a minor surgical procedure. The patient is discharged home later the same day to be followed by the primary care physician. This is coded
   a. 99218, 99217
   b. 99221, 99238
   c. 99234
   d. 99234, 99238

9. An OB-GYN counsels a group of teenagers regarding STDs and their prevention. Session lasts 30 minutes. This is coded
   a. 99401
   b. 99402
   c. 99411
   d. 99411-21

10. A construction worker was seen in the ED for acute eye pain associated with probable steel shaving in the affected eye; the pain is now gone. This is coded
   a. 99281
   b. 99282
   c. 99283
   d. 99284

REVIEW QUESTIONS

1. The CPT E/M guidelines define a new patient as one who has not received professional services from the physician or another physician of the same specialty in the same group practice within the past _____ years.

2. List the three key components of documentation requirement in order to assign an E/M code.

   _____

   _____

   _____

3. Which series of E/M codes are selected for second opinions that may be sought by the patient and/or family, and the physician does not assume the care of the patient?
   a. 99201–99205
   b. 99218–99220
   c. 99241–99245
   d. 99251–99255

4. What criteria are required in the time element of selecting critical care codes?

_____

_____

_____

5. Emergency room visits are coded the Emergency Department section of Evaluation and Management. What section is used to code visits to Urgent/Immediate Care Centers? _____

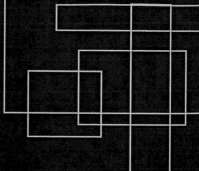

Chapter 6
Anesthesia and General Surgery

Anesthesia Services

All anesthesia services are reported using the five-digit CPT code (00100–01999) plus the addition of a two-digit physical status modifier (P1–P6) to indicate the patient's state of health when undergoing the anesthesia. These modifiers are listed in the Anesthesia Guidelines of CPT. These codes include preoperative and postoperative visits by the anesthesiologist, care during the procedure, monitoring of vital signs, and any fluid administration. Anesthesia codes are assigned based upon the body site for the operation and not on the type of anesthesia administered.

When anesthesia services are provided under difficult circumstances, such as the age of the patient or unusual risks, a five-digit code must be added. This is referred to as Qualifying Circumstances, which is also located in the Anesthesia Guidelines of CPT.

CPT codes for sedation with or without analgesia (conscious sedation) are listed in the Medicine section. CPT code 99141 is used for intravenous, intramuscular, or inhalation sedation. CPT code 99142 is used for oral, rectal, and/or intranasal sedation.

Coding Exercises

Exercise 1

Assign the CPT code for each of the following anesthesia services.

1. Water bath lithotripsy   _____

2. Amniocentesis   _____

3. Diagnostic arthroscopy of shoulder joint   _____

4. Anal fissurectomy   _____

5. Vaginal hysterectomy   _____

6. Corneal transplant   _____

7. Total hip arthroplasty   _____

8. Bilateral vasectomy   _____

9. Gastric bypass for morbid obesity   _____

10. Continuous epidural, labor and delivery   _____

Exercise 2

Assign the CPT anesthesia code and the physical status modifier.

1. Blepharoplasty, patient with Type II diabetes, controlled   _____

2. Breast reduction, healthy patient, no complaints   _____

3. Needle biopsy of thyroid, hypertensive patient   _____

4. Amputation, ankle and foot, of a diabetic patient with gangrene and severe vascular disease   _____

5. Harrington rod procedure for scoliosis, healthy patient   _____

6. Transurethral resection of the prostate, hx. of CVA   _____

7. Heart/lung transplant, severe coronary artery disease   _____

8. Debridement of burn to hands and arms, 4 percent total body surface, of a diabetic patient   _____

9. Transvenous pacemaker insertion, sinus bradycardia   _____

10. Application of cast to lower leg, healthy patient   _____

Coding for Anesthesia and General Surgery—Modifiers

CPT standard modifiers may be used with anesthesia codes. These are:

-22 *Unusual procedural service*—used with rare, unusual, or variable anesthesia services.

-23 *Unusual anesthesia service*—used when a general anesthesia is used in a procedure that requires either no anesthesia or local anesthesia.

-32 *Mandated service*—used when a procedure is a mandated service, such as a PPO, third-party payer, governmental, legislative, or a regulatory requirement.

-47 *Anesthesia by surgeon*—used when regional or general anesthesia is provided by the surgeon, not for services performed by anesthesiologists, anesthetists, or supervised by surgeons.

-51 *Multiple procedures*—used to identify a second procedure or multiple procedures performed during the same operation.

-53 *Discontinued procedure*—used when the procedure is discontinued after anesthesia has been administered but before the incision is made, due to extenuating circumstances or conditions that threaten the health and well-being of the patient.

Note: Modifier -53 may not be used to report the elective cancellation of a procedure prior to administration of the patient's anesthesia and/or surgical preparation in the operating suite.

Coding Exercises

Assign the CPT code for the following anesthesia services. Assign any physical status or CPT modifiers, and add-on codes for qualifying circumstances.

1. Plastic repair for cleft lip, 6-month-old infant   _____

2. Emergency appendectomy, 52-year-old female in otherwise healthy patient   _____

3. Bilateral orchiopexy in hypertensive patient, discontinued after anesthesia is induced due to severe hypertension   _____

4. Physiological support for harvesting organs from brain-dead patient for donor purposes   _____

5. Major abdominal vessel procedure for patient with severe arteriosclerotic cardiovascular disease, life-threatening _____

6. Amputation of ankle and foot in an 85-year-old male, severely diabetic _____

AAPC Certification Review

Select or assign the proper CPT code.

1. A 38-year-old female diagnosed with multiple sclerosis undergoes closed reduction of the right humerus.
   a. 01810-P2
   b. 01820-P3
   c. 01830-P4
   d. 01860-P2

2. A laparoscopic cholecystectomy is performed on a 45-year-old with benign hypertension.
   a. 00700-P2
   b. 00790-P2
   c. 00800-P2
   d. 00840-P3

3. A 32-year-old female with three children undergoes a tubal ligation. Her health is good.
   a. 00840-P1
   b. 00848-P1
   c. 00851-P1
   d. 00940-P1

4. A 78-year-old patient diagnosed with carcinoma of the prostate undergoes a transurethral resection of prostate (TURP).
   a. 00910-99100
   b. 00912-99100
   c. 00914-99100
   d. 00916-99100

5. A patient has a routine colonoscopy using Versed IV for conscious sedation/anesthesia. The code for the anesthesia is
   a. 00810
   b. 45378
   c. 99141
   d. 99142

6. A 55-year-old female diagnosed with early rheumatoid arthritis undergoes anal fistulectomy.
   a. 00810-P2
   b. 00902-P2
   c. 00904-P2
   d. 01432-P3

7. A 16-year-old female with scoliosis undergoes insertion of Harrington rods. She is in good health otherwise.
   a. 00600-P1
   b. 00620-P1
   c. 00640-P1
   d. 00670-P1

8. Lesion removed from left upper thigh requiring regional IV administration of local anesthesia; patient is NIDDM.
   a. 00300-P2
   b. 00400-P2
   c. 01995-P2
   d. 01999-P2

REVIEW QUESTIONS

1. Explain the purpose of assigning a physical status modifier.

   _____

2. List the three methods by which anesthesia can be administered.

   _____

   _____

   _____

3. List the three phases of anesthesia.

   _____

   _____

   _____

4. Describe the responsibilities of the anesthesiologist during the maintenance phase of anesthesia administration. _____

   _____

   _____

5. Codes are assigned from the _____ section of CPT for administering conscious sedation.

General Surgery

General surgery refers to operations performed on the following body systems: respiratory, cardiovascular, hemic and lymphatic, mediastinum and diaphragm, digestive, urinary, male genital, female reproductive, endocrine, nervous, eye and ocular adnexa, and auditory.
   Related types of procedures are grouped in CPT as follows:

- Incisions are procedures that involve cutting into with the ending -otomy or -tomy. Open surgical procedures are performed by creating a surgical incision to access the operative site.
- Excisions are procedures that involve surgical removal with the ending -ectomy. Other terms used in this section include biopsy, resection, or removal.
- Introduction or removal, amputation.
- Repair/revision/reconstruction with the ending -oorhaphy, -oplasty.
- Manipulation or reduction, such as in fractures.
- Fixation or fusion with the ending -opexy.
- Endoscopic or laparoscopic procedures with the ending -oscopy, such as colonoscopy, bronchoscopy, or arthroscopy.

CPT Coding for General Surgery

The following exercises are coded from the respiratory, digestive, urinary, male genital, endocrine, nervous, eye and ocular adnexa, and auditory systems. Exercises for the remaining systems are included in those chapters as related to the textbook.

Coding Exercises

Assign the CPT code for the following, using correct modifiers or add-on codes when indicated.

1. Glossectomy one-fourth portion of tongue   _____
2. Repair of nasal septum   _____
3. I & D of hematoma of epididymis   _____
4. TURP   _____
5. Removal of fecal impaction   _____
6. Colonoscopy to control bleeding   _____
7. Gastric bypass for morbid obesity   _____
8. Exploration of bullet wound to chest   _____
9. Ligation of internal hemorrhoids, single procedure   _____
10. Intraocular lens exchange with ophthalmic endoscope   _____
11. Burr hole for drainage of intracranial abscess   _____
12. Repair initial ventral hernia, reducible, with implantation of mesh   _____
13. Thoracentesis to remove fluid   _____
14. Decompression of carpal tunnel syndrome, left wrist   _____
15. Circumcision of newborn, clamp   _____
16. Removal of impacted cerumen, both ears   _____
17. Laparoscopic orchiectomy   _____
18. Nephrectomy, unilateral, open from living donor   _____
19. Cryotherapy of corneal lesion, left eye   _____
20. Total right lobectomy of liver   _____
21. Emergency endotracheal intubation   _____
22. Laparoscopic appendectomy   _____
23. Removal of bean from nose   _____
24. Cholecystectomy with appendectomy   _____
25. Control and packing of epistaxis, anterior   _____

ICD-9-CM Coding for General Surgery

The following exercises are diagnoses, symptoms, or disorders related to the respiratory, digestive, urinary, male genital, endocrine, nervous, eye and ocular adnexa, and auditory systems. Exercises for the remaining systems are included in those chapters as related to the textbook.

Coding Exercises

Assign the ICD-9-CM code for the following exercises.

1. Crohn's disease   _____

2. Fecal impaction   _____

3. Foreign body in ear canal   _____

4. Deviation of nasal septum, acquired   _____

5. Gunshot wound to external chest   _____

6. Nosebleed   _____

7. Nystagmus   _____

8. Internal bleeding hemorrhoids   _____

9. Pleural effusion   _____

10. Carpal tunnel syndrome   _____

11. Impacted cerumen   _____

12. Acute appendicitis with peritonitis   _____

13. Chronic hepatitis Type B   _____

14. Testicular carcinoma   _____

15. Intracranial abscess   _____

16. Morbid obesity   _____

17. Hematoma of epididymis   _____

18. Urinary retention   _____

19. Carcinoma of tongue, posterior third   _____

20. Allergic rhinitis   _____

21. Acute bronchitis with bronchospasm   _____

22. Nontoxic thyroid goiter   _____

23. Cholelithiasis with cholecystitis   _____

24. Retinal hemorrhage   _____

25. Chronic serous otitis media   _____

AAPC Certification Review

1. Blepharoplasty means surgical repair of the
   a. eyelid
   b. forehead
   c. nasal septum
   d. mandible

2. The insertion of tubes to create an artificial opening into the eardrum is a/an
   a. fenestration
   b. sinusotomy
   c. thoracostomy
   d. tympanostomy

3. Incision and drainage of the lacrimal gland is coded
   a. 68400
   b. 68420
   c. 68440
   d. 68500

4. The term cheiloplasty means surgical repair of
   a. eyelid
   b. forehead
   c. lip
   d. tongue

5. A construction worker was seen in the emergency department for acute eye pain associated with a wood splinter entering the left eye. The patient is treated in the ED for repair of a corneal laceration with foreign body. The correct code is
   a. 65205
   b. 65235
   c. 65270
   d. 65275

6. A surgeon performs removal of external hemorrhoids by rubber band hemorrhoidectomy. The correct code is
   a. 46221
   b. 46230
   c. 46250
   d. 46255

7. A surgeon assists with a total abdominal hysterectomy with Marshall-Marchetti-Krantz procedure. The correct code is
   a. 58150-80
   b. 58152-80
   c. 58200-80
   d. 58267-80

8. Circumcision of a 19-year-old male by surgical excision. The correct code is
   a. 54152
   b. 54160
   c. 54161
   d. 54162

9. Destruction of a rectal tumor by electrodessication. The correct code is
   a. 45190
   b. 45308
   c. 45315
   d. 45320

10. Craniotomy to elevate bone flap for subdural implantation of an electrode array for long-term monitoring of seizure activity. The correct code is
    a. 61526
    b. 61531
    c. 61533
    d. 61566

REVIEW QUESTIONS

1. In order to describe a specific circumstance or an unusual event that alters the definition of the procedure, a coder would assign a(n)
   a. fifth digit
   b. modifier
   c. add-on code
   d. E/M code

2. The term manipulation or reduction refers to
   a. amputation
   b. catheters
   c. fractures
   d. hemorrhage

3. Which one of the following procedures requires the patient's age to be considered for assigning the appropriate CPT code?
   a. Gastric restrictive bypass
   b. Intrauterine device insertion
   c. Tonsillectomy
   d. Vasectomy

4. The procedure commonly performed for correction of sleep apnea is
   a. ERCP
   b. GIFT
   c. TURP
   d. UPPP

5. Identify the endoscopic procedures and name the areas of the colon each examines.

   _____   _____

   _____   _____

   _____   _____

Chapter 7
Integumentary System

Chapter 7 discusses the integumentary system, which includes conditions involving skin, hair, and nails, including excision of skin lesions, and burns and wound repair.

Coding Lacerations

The size of a lesion or laceration is measured and coded in centimeters. When the documentation notes the size in inches, this must be converted to centimeters.

1 inch = 2.54 cm

Coding Exercises

Convert the inches to centimeters, then assign the correct CPT code.

1. Excision, 1-inch benign lesion, left leg   _____   _____

2. Excision, 1/2-inch malignant lesion, finger   _____   _____

3. Simple repair of a 2-inch laceration, rt. foot   _____   _____

4. Intermediate repair of a 5-inch laceration of back   _____   _____

5. Layer closure of a 3-inch wound of the neck   _____   _____

6. Repair of laceration, 2.0 cm, anterior 2/3 of tongue   _____   _____

Other codes for integumentary system:

7. Hair transplant, 21 punch grafts   _____

8. Simple blepharoplasty, right upper lid   _____

9. I & D hematoma, left hand   _____

10. Aspiration, breast cyst, right breast   _____

11. Wound suture, 3/4-inch right hand, 1/2-inch left foot   _____

12. Lipectomy, right buttock   _____

13. Simple right shoulder biopsy, single skin lesion   _____

14. Excision of malignant 1/2-inch lesion, neck   _____

15. Debridement of subcutaneous tissue for infection of foreskin of penis   _____

Coding Burns

Burns are coded by site, depth, or degree, and/or percentage of the body burned.

Depth or degree:

First degree burn	superficial, involving the epidermis. Characterized by redness, hypersensitivity, and sometimes pain.
Second degree burn	partial thickness, involving the dermis and epidermis. Characterized by redness, blistering, edema, and pain.
Third degree burn	full thickness, involving all three areas of the skin. Sensory nerves are destroyed and all sensation to pinprick is lost in the burned area.
Fourth degree burn	deep necrosis; life-threatening. Causes charring of the skin to the bone (e.g., electrical burns).
Fifth degree burn	Bone visibly damaged, probably amputation.

Coding Exercises

Code the following from ICD-9-CM.

1. Second degree burn, rt. upper arm and shoulder

   _____ _____ _____

2. Third degree burn, trunk, 35 percent body surface

   _____ _____

3. Burn of mouth, pharynx, and esophagus

   _____ _____ _____

4. Blisters on back of hand and mouth

   _____ _____ _____

5. Erythema on forearm and elbow

   _____ _____ _____

6. First degree burns of face and both eyes involving cornea, eyelids, nose, cheeks, and lips

   _____

7. Severe sunburn arms and shoulders

   _____

AAPC Certification Review

Code the following exercises from ICD-9-CM as indicated.

1. What is the procedure where foreign material or contaminated tissue is removed from a wound, infected lesion, or trauma site, in order to clean and expose the surrounding healthy tissue?
   a. Biopsy
   b. Cryosurgery
   c. Debridement
   d. Incision and drainage

2. When a decision for surgery is dependent upon the biopsy results during the same session, what modifier is also coded with the biopsy service?

   a. -25

   b. -57

   c. -58

   d. -59

3. A patient with diabetes mellitus Type II is treated for a decubitus ulcer of the sacral area at a nursing facility.

   a. 99313; 250.00; 785.4

   b. 99313; 250.80; 707.03

   c. 99322; 250.80; 707.03

   d. 99343; 250.80; 707.83

4. A patient suffered a minor puncture injury to the finger when removing a staple at the office. Five days later he is treated for cellulitis of the finger with intravenous antibiotics.

   a. 681.00

   b. 681.02

   c. 682

   d. 682.8

5. A patient undergoes excision of an abscessed pilonidal cyst.

   a. 685.0; 11770

   b. 685.0; 11771

   c. 685.0; 11772

   d. 685.1; 11771

6. A patient is seen by a podiatrist for a "sore" on the right little toe. The "sore" is diagnosed as a hard corn deformity and undergoes paring of the lesion.

   a. 700; 11055

   b. 700; 11200

   c. 700; 11305

   d. 709.9; 11055

7. A patient is seen in the office for redness and irritation of the left eyelid. The diagnosis is contact dermatitis. The patient returns for recheck one week later and now has developed cellulitis of the area.

   a. 373.32; 373.13

   b. 373.32; 379.93

   c. 379.93; 373.13

   d. 379.93; 373.32; 373.13

8. Escharotomy performed for a patient with deep third degree burn of the right foot with necrosis. The patient also has Type I adult onset diabetes mellitus, uncontrolled.

   a. 250.00; 945.32; 16035

   b. 250.03; 945.42; 16035

   c. 250.03; 945.30; 16035

   d. 250.03; 945.52; 16035

9. A 15-year-old female receives a superficial burn to the forehead and cheeks from a tanning bed.

   a. 692.71; E926.2

   b. 692.82; E926.2

   c. 941.07; E926.2

   d. 941.17; E926.2

10. A patient is seen in the office by her primary care physician for removal of six skin tags on the back of her neck. During the procedure, she complains of feeling lightheaded. Her blood pressure reveals an elevated reading of 182/96. She has no previous history of hypertension. The physician feels the elevation may be due to her anxiety about the procedure today. The B/P will be checked weekly for the next month to monitor the readings. What codes are reported for this encounter?

    a. 11057; 99213-25
    b. 11200; 99213-25
    c. 11200; 99213-51
    d. 11200; 99214

REVIEW QUESTIONS

1. Which depth of a burn involves all layers of the skin with destruction of nerve cells?

    a. First degree
    b. Second degree
    c. Third degree
    d. Fourth degree

2. Which burn is characterized by redness, hypersensitivity, and some pain?

    a. First degree
    b. Second degree
    c. Third degree
    d. Fourth degree

3. Which one of the following would be classified as a fourth degree burn?

    a. Blistering of skin due to burn to hand while cooking
    b. Erythema of face from exposure to steam
    c. Charring of skin to the bone with deep necrosis from contact with an electrical wire
    d. Destruction of sensory nerves from burn while extinguishing flames from a blanket

4. List the organs/accessory organs included in the integumentary system:

    _____

    _____

    _____

    _____

5. What is the purpose of the Rule of Nines?

    a. To calculate the percentage of total body surface affected in a burn patient
    b. To determine the depth or degree of the burn
    c. To determine if a lesion is benign or malignant
    d. To assist in conversion of the size of a wound

Chapter 8
Orthopedics

Orthopedics is a medical specialty concerned with the prevention, investigation, diagnosis, and treatment of diseases, disorders, and injuries of the musculoskeletal system. This medical specialty is a major provider in the treatment of work-related injuries, motor vehicle accidents, and falls. In these instances, assigning E-codes in addition to the diagnosis code will describe the cause of the injury in order to determine liability for the charges, such as Workers' Compensation, homeowners, or auto insurance.

Fractures involve the musculoskeletal system and are the result of a trauma or accident but there are also pathological fractures. These are fractures that occur in bones that are weakened by disease. They are usually spontaneous but sometimes occur in connection with a slight trauma that ordinarily would not result in a fracture in healthy bone. There are many underlying causes for pathological fractures, including osteoporosis, metastatic tumor of the bone, osteomyelitis, Paget's disease, disuse atrophy, hyperparathyroidism, and nutritional or congenital disorders.

Dislocation, also called luxation, is a disarrangement of two or more bones from their articular processes. An incomplete dislocation is called a subluxation. When a dislocation is associated with a fracture at the same location, code only the fracture. It is possible to have a fracture and dislocation of the same bone. When the fracture and dislocation have occurred at different sites, two codes can be assigned.

Coding Exercises

Code the following conditions using Volumes 1 and 2 of ICD-9-CM.

1. Acute and chronic gouty arthritis   _____

2. Chronic nodular rheumatoid arthritis w/polyneuropathy   _____   _____

3. Herniated intervertebral disc, L4-5   _____

4. Chronic lumbosacral sprain   _____

5. Primary osteoarthritis of hip   _____

6. Osteomyelitis of left distal femur due to diabetes   _____   _____

7. Adhesive capsulitis, left shoulder   _____

8. Recurrent dislocation of patella   _____

9. Multiple compression fractures of vertebrae due to senile
   osteoporosis   _____   _____

10. Cervical spondylosis, C5-6, C6-7   _____

11. Fracture, rt. tibia, in person with AIDS   _____   _____

12. Fracture of left ilium in patient with Type II diabetes mellitus _____ _____

13. Greenstick fx. third digit, right foot _____

14. Multiple fractures, right femur, distal end _____

15. Open fracture maxilla _____

Coding Exercises

Code the following procedures from CPT.

1. Application of figure-of-eight cast _____

2. Surgical exploration of gunshot wound to the chest with debridement and removal of the bullet _____

3. Arthroscopy of shoulder with rotator cuff repair _____

4. Aspiration of ganglion cyst of wrist _____

5. Open treatment of clavicular fracture with internal fixation _____

6. Arthroscopy, knee, surgical, for infection, lavage, and drainage _____

7. Removal of nail from foot, deep _____

8. Treatment of spontaneous hip dislocation by splint _____

9. Amputation of metatarsal of great toe _____

10. Excision of tumor of thigh, intramuscular _____

11. Excision of benign tumor of the scapula with allograft _____

12. Insertion of Harrington rod in patient with scoliosis _____

13. Cartilage graft of the nasal septum _____

14. Application of cranial halo of underdeveloped child _____

15. Arthroscopy of elbow with limited debridement to remove gravel _____

AAPC Certification Review

1. A patient is seen and evaluated for osteoarthritis of the right knee. Aspiration of the knee revealed no fluid. The site was injected with 2 mL of hylan G-F 20 (Synvisc) without complication. The correct codes are
   a. 715.06; 20610
   b. 715.96; 20605
   c. 715.96; 20610
   d. 716.96; 20610

2. A patient diagnosed with Dupuytren's contracture of the left hand undergoes a palmar fasciotomy using open technique. The correct codes are
   a. 728.6; 26040-RT
   b. 728.6; 26045-RT
   c. 728.6; 26121-RT
   d. 728.6; 26123-RT

3. Which one of the following is an example of an open fracture?
   a. Comminuted
   b. Compound
   c. Greenstick
   d. Impacted

4. What are the two most common procedures associated with fractures?
   a. Incision and drainage
   b. Luxation and subluxation
   c. Open and closed
   d. Reduction and fixation

5. A 12-year-old boy is seen in the ED following a fall from his bicycle. An x-ray shows a closed fracture of the greater tuberosity of the left humerus. The correct codes are
   a. 812.03; E826.1
   b. 812.09; E826.1
   c. 812.13; E826.1
   d. 812.20; E826.1

6. A 75-year-old female is diagnosed with a pathological fracture of the hip secondary to Paget's disease. The correct code(s) is(are)
   a. 731.0
   b. 731.0; 733.14
   c. 733.14
   d. 820.8

7. A patient diagnosed with acquired trigger thumb undergoes tendon sheath incision release surgery. The correct codes are
   a. 26055; 727.03
   b. 26055; 756.89
   c. 26060; 756.89
   d. 26160; 727.03

8. Which one of the following is considered an autoimmune disease/disorder of the musculoskeletal system?
   a. Osteoarthritis
   b. Rheumatoid arthritis
   c. Schmorl's nodes
   d. Scoliosis

9. A new patient is seen in the office complaining of weakness of the right side of her face with some paralysis. Examination of the patient reveals a diagnosis of Bell's palsy. The patient's overall health is otherwise good. The correct codes are
   a. 99201; 351.0
   b. 99211; 351.0
   c. 99201; 780.79; 351.0
   d. 99202; 780.79; 351.0

10. A patient had been seen in the office initially for recurrent ganglion cyst of the right wrist. Initial treatment had been an injection into the affected area. Today the cyst is surgically removed in the ambulatory surgical center. The correct codes are
   a. 25110; 727.43
   b. 25111; 727.43
   c. 25112; 727.43
   d. 25112; 727.49

REVIEW QUESTIONS

1. List some of the diseases, disorders, and injuries treated by an orthopedic practice.

_____

_____

_____

_____

_____

_____

_____

2. Name three diseases/disorders that may cause a pathological fracture.

_____

_____

_____

3. An "open" fracture means the skin is broken. What five descriptive terms are listed in ICD-9-CM to define an open fracture?

_____

_____

_____

_____

_____

4. A "closed" fracture means the skin is not broken through and bone is not protruding. What seven descriptive terms are listed in ICD-9-CM to define a closed fracture?

_____   _____

_____   _____

_____   _____

_____

5. What incidents may require assigning an E-code to the diagnosis code?

_____

_____

_____

_____

_____

Chapter 9
Cardiology and Cardiovascular System

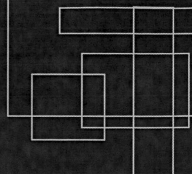

The cardiovascular system specializes in diseases of the heart and vessels. Specialists in the diagnosis and treatment of the heart include the cardiologist who is the physician specializing in cardiology and the cardiothoracic surgeon who specializes in surgical procedures of the heart and chest. Other physicians utilize codes and procedures related to cardiology, such as electrocardiograms, CPR, and other therapeutic services. Conditions treated by many physicians such as hypertension and hypercholesterolemia are included in the cardiovascular system.

The anatomical structure and the function of the heart are essential to coding cardiac procedures and disorders. Understanding the terminology of the heart is important, including the abbreviations and acronyms.

Coding Exercises

Code the following diagnoses, symptoms, and disorders from ICD-9-CM.

1. Angina pectoris with benign hypertension _____ _____

2. Atrial fibrillation _____

3. Mitral valve insufficiency, congenital _____

4. AMI inferoposterior wall, initial _____

5. Abdominal aortic aneurysm _____

6. Chest pain, R/O AMI _____

7. Family hx. of ischemic heart disease _____

8. Hypertensive heart disease _____

9. CHF with atrial fibrillation _____ _____

10. Chronic rheumatic pericarditis _____

Coding Exercises

Code the following procedures and services from CPT.

1. Insertion of dual chamber pacemaker _____

2. Routine venipuncture _____

3. Elecrocardiogram, 12 leads, with interpretation/ report _____

4. Post-op hemorrhage of chest, exploration _____

5. Pericardiotomy to remove blood clot _____

6. Pulmonary valve replacement _____

7. 2D transthoracic echocardiography with treadmill with Cardiolyte for stress induction, complete _____ _____

8. Insertion and placement of Swan-Ganz catheter for monitoring _____

9. Heart-lung transplant with recipient cardiectomy/ pneumonectomy _____

10. Transluminal balloon angioplasty, aortic vessel _____

AAPC Certification Review

1. A 45-year-old male is admitted to the coronary unit with acute MI of the inferoposterior wall, initial, with congestive heart failure and hypertension. The ICD-9-CM codes for this admission are
   a. 410.21, 428.0, 401.9
   b. 410.30, 428.0, 401.9
   c. 410.31, 428.0, 401.9
   d. 410.41, 428.0, 401.9

2. A 32-year-old patient is in the office with the complaint of a fast, racing heart rate. The EKG shows premature ventricular contractions. The patient was last seen by this physician four years ago and treated for hypertension. Blood pressure today is elevated at 192/94. This is coded
   a. 99203, 93000, 427.69, 401.9
   b. 99203, 93000, 427.69, 401.0
   c. 99213, 93000, 427.69, 401.9
   d. 99213. 93000, 427.69, 401.0

3. Referring to question 2, this patient is referred to a cardiologist for consultation, evaluation, and treatment recommendations for the PVCs. An EKG is performed that again shows the PVCs. The patient will be monitored for 24 hours by a Holter monitor producing a full printout, recording, analysis, report, physician review, and interpretation. This is coded
   a. 99204, 93000, 93230
   b. 99243, 93000, 93230
   c. 99253, 93000, 93230
   d. 99263, 93000, 93230

4. Tachycardia means
   a. cardiac insufficiency
   b. fast heart rate
   c. irregular heart rate
   d. slow heart rate

5. A 39-year-old female is referred to a cardiologist with a diagnosis of mitral valve prolapse. A cardiac stress test done previously at the hospital is reviewed and interpreted by the cardiologist during the consultation visit in the office. Her health has been good otherwise. This is coded

   a. 99203, 93015, 424.0

   b. 99242, 93015, 424.0

   c. 99242, 93018, 424.0

   d. 99262, 93018, 424.0

6. A 49-year-old male was seen in the emergency department for chest pain. He had been seen in the hospital three months ago for a myocardial infarction. This is coded

   a. 410.92

   b. 786.50, 411.1

   c. 785.50, 414.8

   d. 414.8

7. A patient complains of difficulty breathing and shortness of air with exertion. It is noted by the physician she does have severe edema in the lower extremities. She is hypertensive with an elevated blood pressure reading today. Diagnoses documented for today's visit are congestive heart failure and hypertension. This is coded

   a. 398.91

   b. 402.91

   c. 428.0, 401.9

   d. 786.05, 782.3, 401.9

8. A patient is admitted to the cardiac unit with acute MI, initial, of the inferolateral wall and a third degree AV block. This is coded

   a. 410.20, 426.0

   b. 410.21, 426.0

   c. 410.21, 426.6

   d. 410.21, 426.10

9. A patient undergoes repair of a thoracoabdominal aorta aneurysm with graft and cardiopulmonary bypass. This is coded

   a. 33860, 441.7

   b. 33877, 441.4

   c. 33877, 441.7

   d. 33877, 441.03

10. A patient is admitted to the hospital with bronchopneumonia and sick sinus syndrome. Patient will be followed daily by this physician until discharged. This is coded

   a. 99218, 485, 427.81

   b. 99221, 485, 427.81

   c. 99221, 486, 427.81

   d. 99231, 485, 427.89

REVIEW QUESTIONS

Identify each of the following cardiac acronyms.

1. CABG   _____

2. BBB   _____

3. PAD   _____

4. MVP   _____

5. PTCA   _____

6. ASHD   _____

7. HTN   _____

8. CHF   _____

9. CAD   _____

10. CPR   _____

Match each of the following terms with the correct definition.

_____ 1. Atrium   a. Blood flow obstruction

_____ 2. Ventricles   b. Middle layer of heart

_____ 3. Tricuspid   c. Outside covering of heart

_____ 4. Bicuspid   d. Lower chambers of heart

_____ 5. SA node   e. Upper chambers of heart

_____ 6. Myocardium   f. Conductor for electrical impulses

_____ 7. Pericardium   g. AV valves

_____ 8. Endocardium   h. Natural pacemaker of heart

_____ 9. Bundle of His   i. Mitral valves

_____ 10. Occlusion   j. Innermost layer of heart

Chapter 10
OB/GYN

Female Genital System: Maternity Care and Delivery

The following subsection of CPT-4 covers procedures performed on the female genital system and for maternity care and delivery. In the female genital system, codes for body site and for in vitro fertilization are listed by the type of procedure. Note that in some descriptors, the terms salpingo- and oophor- are used, and in others, tube(s) and ovary(s). The terms "salpingo-oophorectomy" and "removal of the ovary and its fallopian tube" have the same meaning.

The maternity care and delivery codes have a unique organization. They are grouped as follows: antepartum services; excision; introduction; repair; vaginal delivery, antepartum, and postpartum care (normal uncomplicated cases); cesarean delivery; delivery after previous cesarean delivery; abortion; and other procedures.

The Obstetric Package

The guidelines for maternity care/delivery describe the obstetric package of services normally provided for uncomplicated cases. The package consists of antepartum care, delivery, and postpartum care, as described. Before coding obstetrical services, study these notes carefully to avoid unbundling. Understanding the obstetric package also permits correct reporting of those services that are not part of the package and that can be coded separately.

Coding Exercises

Code the following procedures from CPT.

1. Complete radical vulvectomy   _____

2. D & C, postpartum hemorrhage   _____

3. Total abdominal hysterectomy   _____

4. Subtotal hysterectomy   _____

5. Insertion of IUD   _____

6. Diagnostic hysteroscopy   _____

7. Bilateral complete salpingo-oophorectomy   _____

8. Radical abdominal hysterectomy w/salpingo-oophorectomy   _____

9. Vaginectomy and complete removal of vaginal wall   _____

10. Routine obstetric care/vaginal delivery   _____

11. Episiotomy by assisting physician   _____

12. Miscarriage surgically completed in first trimester   _____

13. Chromotubation of oviduct including materials   _____   _____

14. Five visits for antepartum care only   _____

15. Bilateral drainage of ovarian cysts by abdominal approach   _____

Complications of Pregnancy, Childbirth, and Puerperium

Codes in this chapter of ICD-9-CM classify conditions that are involved with pregnancy, childbirth, and puerperium. Many categories require a fifth-digit subclassification based on when the complications occur (referred to as the episode of care), either before birth (antepartum), during, or after birth (postpartum).

These codes are assigned to the conditions of the mother only, not of the infant. They cover the course of pregnancy and childbirth from conception through the puerperium, which is the six-week period following delivery.

Coding Exercises

Code the following from Volumes 1 and 2 of ICD-9-CM.

1. Ectopic pregnancy   _____

2. Incomplete spontaneous abortion w/complications   _____

3. Hemorrhage in pregnancy at 18 weeks   _____

4. False labor   _____

5. Essential hypertension complicating pregnancy   _____

6. Gestational diabetes   _____

7. Delivery of triplets   _____   _____

8. Uterine death of delivered late-term fetus   _____

9. Rh incompatibility   _____

10. Nipple fissure in fourth week after childbirth   _____

11. Normal delivery of single liveborn   _____   _____

12. Normal delivery of liveborn twins   _____   _____

13. Normal delivery of quadruplets, three liveborn, one stillborn   _____   _____

Conditions Originating in the Perinatal Period

Using ICD-9-CM, code the following conditions of the fetus or newborn infant (neonate), which covers the perinatal period (the period shortly before birth until 28 days following delivery). When the hospitalization that results in the birth is to be coded, these codes are seconday to codes from categories V30 through V39. Note the use of the fourth digit to designate the birth location and of the fifth digit to specify hospital births.

Coding Exercises

1. Fetal alcohol syndrome _____

2. Fetus affected by mother's malnutrition _____

3. Neonatal hepatitis _____

4. Respiratory distress syndrome _____

5. Convulsions in newborn _____

6. Hospital birth of living infant, premature, weighs 2000 grams _____

7. Full-term birth in hospital of living male child, delivered by
    cesarean section, w/neonatal transient hyperthyroidism _____

8. Premature birth of female twins, first child delivered in
    ambulance en route to hospital, second child delivered in hospital _____

AAPC Certification Review

Select the proper ICD-9-CM codes.

1. A pregnant patient is treated for an acute urinary tract infection due to E. coli bacteria.
    a. 646.50; 599.0; 041.4
    b. 646.60; 599.0; 041.4
    c. 646.61; 599.0; 041.4
    d. 646.63; 599.0; 041.4

2. A pregnant woman is admitted to the hospital for vaginal bleeding following a fall at home. She is at
    20 weeks gestation.
    a. 646.33; 641.83
    b. 646.30; 641.90
    c. 646.33; 641.93
    d. 646.33; 666.13

3. A woman in her 22nd week of pregnancy is evaluated by her OB for excessive vomiting caused by
    acute gastroenteritis.
    a. 643.23; 558.9
    b. 643.80; 558.9
    c. 643.83; 558.9
    d. 643.93; 558.9

4. The physician successfully performs resuscitation on a newborn infant with cardiac distress during
    delivery.
    a. 99432
    b. 99435
    c. 99436
    d. 99440

5. A patient consults a surgeon for opinion for recommended hysterectomy by her primary care physician. This visit is coded a/an
   a. risk factor counseling
   b. expanded problem-focused visit for a new patient
   c. followup consultation
   d. initial office consultation

6. A 33-year-old patient is seen for an annual pelvic examination including Pap smear. She is complaining of menorrhagia since her last exam one year ago. Pelvic exam is normal. A CBC performed in the office today reveals iron deficiency anemia.
   a. V72.31, 626.2, 280.9
   b. V76.2, 626.2, 280.9
   c. V721.31, 626.2, 281.9
   d. V76.2, 626.2, 281.9

7. A 39-year-old female undergoes a vaginal hysterectomy with Marshall-Marchetti-Krantz procedure; uterus weighs 255 grams.
   a. 58267
   b. 58270
   c. 58290
   d. 58293

8. Patient is seen for excision of Bartholin's cyst.
   a. 56420
   b. 56440
   c. 56740
   d. 57135

9. Tubal ligation of patient, vaginal approach, bilateral, for sterilization purpose.
   a. 58600; V26.51
   b. 58605; V26.51
   c. 58600-50; V25.2
   d. 58605-50; V26.51

10. When coding and billing for obstetrical services in a normal, uncomplicated pregnancy, a global package concept is used, which includes
    a. antepartum, delivery, and postpartum care
    b. Pap smear, prenatal panel, delivery
    c. pregnancy test, antepartum, and postpartum care
    d. pregnancy test, monthly exams, delivery

REVIEW QUESTIONS

1. The term gestation means
   a. the duration of pregnancy
   b. the completion of delivery
   c. the beginning of the menstrual function

2. The obstetric package for uncomplicated pregnancy and delivery include three services. They are:

_____

_____

_____

3. The term puerperium refers to
    a. period of time before delivery
    b. period of time after delivery
    c. recovery time after delivery for the uterus to return to normal
    d. beginning of menstrual function

4. Name the internal organs of the female reproductive system.

_____

_____

_____

_____

5. List four sexually transmitted diseases.

_____

_____

_____

_____

Chapter 11
Radiology, Pathology, and Laboratory

Radiology

Radiology section of CPT contains five categories of services:

- *Diagnostic imaging or x-rays* include CAT/CT scans, MRI, mammography, and angiography.
- *Diagnostic ultrasound* uses sound waves to create an image: A-mode, M-mode, B-scan, and real-time.
- *Radiation oncology* uses radiation: measured in rads, based on number of areas, ports, and blocks. Radiation materials implanted directly into an anatomical site using ribbons and sources is called brachytherapy, which is often used in the treatment of breast cancer.
- *Nuclear medicine* uses radioactive materials within the body to diagnose or use in therapeutic testing, such as a stress test.
- *Interventional radiology* is a combination of both a surgical procedure and a radiological service.

Radiology CPT codes are used when radiological services are performed by the physician or under the supervision of a physician. A modifier or specified code referred to as the professional component of the service may be assigned if the radiological service was not performed by the physician but was read and interpreted by the physician. Modifier -26 is used to indicate the physician provided the professional portion of the test only; modifier TC is used to indicate that only the technical component was provided. When the CPT code includes "supervision and interpretation," it cannot be used for providing the technical portion of the test.

Coding Exercises

Assign the correct CPT code to the following exercises.

1. Bilateral bronchogram _____

2. Chest x-ray, anterior and lateral _____

3. GI series with small bowel and air studies, without KUB _____

4. Initial screening mammogram, bilateral _____

5. Cervical MRI, no contrast _____

6. Complete obstetrical B-scan, first trimester _____

7. Bilateral carotid angiogram, supervision/interpretation _____

8. DXA scan for bone density of hips, pelvis, spine _____

9. X-ray for TMJ, right _____

10. X-ray tibia and fibula, left leg, two views _____

AAPC Certification Review

Select the proper code.

1. A patient has a complete chest x-ray, four views, to recheck status of bronchopneumonia.
   a. 71010
   b. 71020
   c. 71030
   d. 71035

2. A patient with a complaint of diarrhea alternating with constipation has a barium enema with air contrast of the colon.
   a. 74246
   b. 74270
   c. 74280
   d. 74283

3. A patient undergoes cardiac MRI for velocity flow mapping.
   a. 75552
   b. 75554
   c. 75555
   d. 75556

4. A 56-year-old female has her annual routine mammogram on October 5. After the films are reviewed, a small nodule is noted in the left breast. On October 21, a repeat mammogram is performed with a computer aided detection image study of the left breast. What codes would be assigned for the procedures done on October 21?
   a. 76090, 76082
   b. 76091, 76082
   c. 76092, 76083
   d. 76092, 76090

5. An ultrasound of the neck is performed to check diagnosis of hypothyroidism.
   a. 76536
   b. 78000
   c. 78006
   d. 78010

6. A patient diagnosed with gastroparesis has a gastric emptying study.
   a. 78261
   b. 78262
   c. 78264
   d. 78299

7. PET scan for tumor imaging of the chest is performed.
   a. 71550
   b. 78580
   c. 78811
   d. 78814

8. An ultrasound is performed on a 44-year-old female to check for ovarian cysts. The patient is not pregnant.
   a. 76801
   b. 76805
   c. 76830
   d. 76856

9. A patient has symptoms of temporomandibular joint disorder. X-ray is made, open and closed views, bilateral.
   a. 70328
   b. 70330
   c. 70332
   d. 70336

10. The driver of a motorcycle involved in an MVA is seen in the emergency department for possible fracture of the tibia and fibula.
    a. 73590
    b. 73595
    c. 73700
    d. 73706

REVIEW QUESTIONS

1. Name the four categories of radiology coding located in the CPT code book.

   _____

   _____

   _____

   _____

2. What does each of the following abbreviations represent?
   MRI _____
   CT   _____
   CAT _____
   PET _____

3. What is modifier -26 used to report? _____

4. Match the area or anatomical site with the correct nuclear medicine scan.
   _____ Osteomyelitis   a. Bone scan
   _____ Kidney function   b. Cardiac scan
   _____ Myocardial infarction   c. Lung scan
   _____ COPD   d. Renal scan
   _____ Ventricular aneurysms
   _____ Osteoporosis

5. Brachytherapy is used in the treatment of what type of carcinoma? _____

Pathology/Laboratory

The Pathology/Laboratory section of CPT includes ordering the test, obtaining and preparing a specimen, the testing process and interpreting results. It is important to know where the service is performed when assigning the code. For example, a patient may be seen in the office for an annual Pap smear, where the specimen is obtained, but sent to pathology for interpretation. The collection of the specimen for preparation to be sent to the lab may be billable by the physician's office, but the outside source would bill for the testing and interpretation of the specimen, assigning a code from the pathology section of CPT. Another example is, a venipuncture code can be assigned for drawing the blood in the office, but if the blood is sent to a lab for testing and reporting, the outside source would bill the patient for this service using laboratory codes from CPT.

Coding Exercises

Assign CPT codes to the following exercises.

1. Urinalysis dipstick, nonautomated, complete, with microscope _____

2. Heavy metal screen _____

3. Urine pregnancy test _____

4. Electrolyte panel _____

5. Fasting glucose, blood, quantitative _____

6. Thyroid stimulating hormone _____

7. Routine prothrombin time _____

8. Autopsy as ordered by coroner _____

9. Pap smear, vaginal/cervical slides, manual, under physician screening _____

10. Stool test for Helicobacter pylori _____

AAPC Certification Review

1. A 49-year-old patient is seen in the office for six-month evaluation of hyperlipidemia. The physician orders blood drawn in the office to be sent to the laboratory to check serum cholesterol, lipoprotein with HDL, and triglycerides. What codes would be assigned for physician billing?
   a. 99212, 36415
   b. 99212, 36415, 80061
   c. 99396, 36415
   d. 99396, 36415, 80061

2. A 19-year-old patient is seen in the office for ABO blood typing and urine pregnancy test. She is an established patient in the practice. What codes would be assigned?
   a. 99202, 86900, 81025
   b. 99212, 86900, 81025
   c. 99212, 86910, 81025
   d. 99212, 86910, 81005

3. A physician orders a comprehensive metabolic panel. In addition, the order includes a CBC and TSH. How would this be coded?
   a. Code the comprehensive metabolic panel and the CBC and TSH individually.
   b. Code a general health panel.
   c. Code a basic metabolic panel and the CBC and TSH individually.
   d. Code a comprehensive metabolic panel.

4. A 69-year-old male has blood drawn in the lab for a Lee and White coagulation study to check level for adjustment of his Coumadin dosage. This is coded
   a. 85300
   b. 85337
   c. 85345
   d. 85348

5. A 32-year-old female is seen in the office for annual pelvic examination with Pap smear. She is a new patient to this office and states she is in good health and has no complaints today. Specimen is obtained for the Pap smear and sent to the laboratory. She will be notified of the results in 10 days. She will return prn. How is this coded for physician billing?
   a. 88147
   b. 88150
   c. 99201
   d. 99385

6. What is the code for a urine culture with quantitative colony count for bacteria?
   a. 87081
   b. 87084
   c. 87086
   d. 87088

7. A patient is seen in the laboratory for a three-hour glucose tolerance test. This is coded
   a. 82946
   b. 82947
   c. 82951
   d. 82952

8. A specimen is received by the laboratory for a semen analysis to check volume, presence, count, and motility of sperm, and differential. This is coded
   a. 89300
   b. 89310
   c. 89320
   d. 89321

9. A blood specimen is received by the laboratory for a creatinine test. This is coded
   a. 82540
   b. 82550
   c. 82565
   d. 82570

10. A patient who is hospitalized has blood drawn for testing of blood gases, including calculated O_2 saturation. This is coded

   a. 82800

   b. 82803

   c. 82805

   d. 82810

Chapter Review

1. What does the term pathology mean? _____

   _____

   _____

2. Name five tests that are designated as waived laboratory tests as defined by CLIA '88 regulations.

   _____

   _____

   _____

   _____

   _____

3. How does a venipunture code differ from any other collection of specimen code?

   _____

   _____

   _____

4. List the tests included in the electrolyte panel.

   _____

   _____

   _____

   _____

5. What do each of the following laboratory abbreviations represent?

   BUN _____

   CBC _____

   TSH _____

   PSA _____

   3-hr GTT _____

   FBS _____

Chapter 12
Medicine

The Medicine section of CPT contains codes for a variety of procedures and services provided by many different types of health care providers. Two basic types of subsections are included: those that are procedure related and those that refer to particular medical specialties, such as physical medicine, ophthalmology, and home health services.

Included in the Medicine section are Special Services, Procedures, and Reports that provide codes for miscellaneous services that are an adjunct to the basic services rendered to indicate the special circumstances under which a basic procedure is performed, such as specimen handling, special insurance reporting forms, and supplies and materials. Always code documented services and procedures provided or performed by a physician. While there are codes for these special circumstances, third-party payers do not always reimburse the provider.

Coding Exercises

Assign CPT codes to the following.

1. Medical testimony   _____

2. MMR, live vaccine, SQ, age 6   _____   _____

3. Injection PCN, IM   _____

4. Percutaneous allergy testing by puncture with allergenic extracts, immediate type reaction, 14 tests   _____

5. Color vision exam, for color-blindness   _____

6. Psychotherapy including patient and family   _____

7. Tympanometry   _____

8. Medical hypnotherapy to stop smoking   _____

9. CPAP   _____

10. Oral polio virus vaccine   _____   _____

11. Rabies immune globulins, IM, age 10   _____   _____

12. Cardiovascular stress test, treadmill, complete _____

13. Spirometry for pulmonary function analysis   _____

14. Completion of insurance claim forms for life insurance application/
    questionnaire   _____

15. Laser treatment for psoriasis, 375 sq cm   _____

AAPC Certification Review

Assign the correct CPT codes for the following scenarios.

1. Gastroesophageal reflux test including placement, recording, analysis, and interpretation for patient
   suspected of GERD.
   a. 91010
   b. 91020
   c. 91034
   d. 91037

2. A new patient, age 55, is seen in the office for an expanded problem-focused exam. He also receives
   pneumococcal and flu vaccines given IM.
   a. 90471, 90472, 90658, 90732
   b. 90471, 90658, 90732, 99202
   c. 90471, 90472, 90658, 90732, 99202
   d. 90471, 90472, 90655, 90732, 99202

3. A patient is given IM injection of Phenergen for nausea and vomiting.
   a. 90772
   b. 90773
   c. 90774
   d. 90799

4. A patient receives assistance in her home for bathing, dressing, and meal preparation.
   a. 99321
   b. 99347
   c. 99509
   d. 99600

5. A patient removed from life-support is evaluated by EEG for cerebral death.
   a. 93235
   b. 95812
   c. 95822
   d. 95824

6. An established patient returns for a routine eye examination on an intermediate level. He has decided
   to be fitted with contact lenses, and the ophthalmologist supervises the fitting and adaptation of the
   lenses. The patient receives a 90-day supply of the prescribed contact lenses.
   a. 92002, 92310
   b. 92012, 92310
   c. 92012, 92314
   d. 92012, 92325

7. Referring to question 6, the patient calls three months later to state he has lost his right contact lens. The office orders a replacement lens for the patient to pick up at the office.
    a. 92310-52
    b. 92311
    c. 92326
    d. 92391

8. An established patient is seen in the office for a follow-up ECG after being seen in the hospital emergency department for chest pain. A 12-lead study is performed, including interpretation and report by the physician. The exam is expanded problem-focused.
    a. 99203, 93000
    b. 99213, 93000
    c. 99213, 93010
    d. 99282, 93233

9. Five patients participating in a group psychotherapy session receive audiotapes provided by the physician.
    a. 90806, 99071
    b. 90846, 99070
    c. 90853, 99071
    d. 90901, 99070

10. A patient is seen in the office for preparation of chemotherapy agent to be administered by IV push in the office, performed on a monthly basis.
    a. 96400, 99213
    b. 96408, 99213
    c. 96410, 99212
    d. 96420, 99213

REVIEW QUESTIONS

1. Which one of the following services would be assigned a code from the Medicine section of CPT?
    a. Hospital admission
    b. Immunizations
    c. Interpretation of radiology report
    d. Nursing facility service

2. Name five subsections located in the Medicine section of CPT.

    _____

    _____

    _____

    _____

    _____

3. In what subsection of Medicine section would you locate codes for polysomnography and sleep studies?

    a. Allergy

    b. Endocrinology

    c. Neurology

    d. Physical Medicine and Rehabilitation

4. Which one of the following medications is an IM antibiotic injection?

    a. Diazepam

    b. Phenergen

    c. Vitamin B-12

    d. Zithromax

5. When coding immunizations, which of the following is correct?

    a. An administration code is assigned in addition to the vaccine code.

    b. An administration code is assigned in addition to the prophylactic code.

    c. An administration code, prophylactic code, and HCPCS codes are assigned.

    d. None of the above

Chapter 13
Billing and Collections

Accuracy and completeness in assigning codes for diagnoses and procedures and linking these codes accurately to indicate the medical necessity are important in the billing, reimbursement, and collections for services rendered in any health care facility. Billing begins with the patient information form completed prior to the patient being seen by the provider. This information should not stop there. It should be checked each time the patient returns to the office so medical and financial records are current and accurate.

Since initial contact begins when the patient calls the office to inquire about a practice and make an appointment, everyone in a medical practice needs to understand patient information necessary to prepare the patient's medical record, establish the patient's account, collect co-pay and co-insurance amounts, and submit claims to third party payers.

The patient information form can be designed to obtain patient information exclusive to a particular practice and/or specialty. Many forms now request cell phone number and e-mail address. Others may ask such questions as the name a patient prefers to be called, such as a nickname, or how did the patient learn about the practice. Information may also include policies on financial arrangements and late charges.

Coding Questions

Match the diagnosis with the procedure to show a valid linkage for medical necessity.

	Diagnosis		Procedure
_____	1. Migraine headache	a.	Colonoscopy
_____	2. Chest pain	b.	Needle biopsy
_____	3. Dysuria	c.	Myringotomy
_____	4. Prostatic hypertrophy	d.	Injection of Demerol & Phenergen
_____	5. Seizure disorder	e.	Ultrasound of gallbladder
_____	6. Epistaxis	f.	Steroid injection
_____	7. Cholecystitis	g.	Urinalysis
_____	8. Positive PPD	h.	Puncture aspiration
_____	9. Type I diabetes mellitus	i.	TURP
_____	10. Pancreatic carcinoma	j.	Chest x-ray
_____	11. Family hx. of colon cancer	k.	Debridement
_____	12. Cystic lesion of breast	l.	Nasal packing
_____	13. Superficial skin abrasion	m.	Blood glucose
_____	14. Chronic otitis media	n.	EKG
_____	15. Bursitis of shoulder	o.	EEG

AAPC Certification Review

1. An established patient is seen in the Digestive Clinic for a detailed consultation for possible GERD. What test would confirm this diagnosis?
   a. 91010
   b. 91020
   c. 91030
   d. 91034

2. A patient is referred to an orthopedic surgeon for evaluation of bursitis, for which she was treated in the past by this physician group. A detailed history and exam is performed. Complete x-rays of the right shoulder confirm the bursitis. An injection of cortisone is administered into the right shoulder bursa. What is the correct code for the injection?
   a. 90772
   b. 90773
   c. 20605
   d. 20610

3. A patient diagnosed with morbid obesity is seen in consultation in the surgeon's office for gastric bypass procedure. He completes the patient registration form for a new patient and presents his insurance card. The visit today is a detailed history and examination. What is the correct E/M code?
   a. 43846
   b. 99203
   c. 99243
   d. 99253

4. When a second opinion is mandated by a third-party payer, what CPT modifier would be added to the E/M code?
   a. -25
   b. -32
   c. -57
   d. -62

5. A patient is prepped for a routine colonoscopy as an outpatient at the ambulatory surgery center. After the IV medications are administered and the scope inserted, the patient has a seizure, and the physician discontinues the procedure. What CPT modifier would be used to indicate this?
   a. -52
   b. -53
   c. -73
   d. -74

6. A patient previously diagnosed with sick sinus syndrome is brought to the emergency room after experiencing tachycardia. Which one of the following would *not* be a procedure related to this diagnosis and symptoms?
   a. 33200
   b. 93000
   c. 93224
   d. 95812

7. A routine screening mammogram is performed on a 44-year-old female with a family history of breast cancer. A two-view film study of each breast is taken. What is the correct CPT code?
   a. 76090-50
   b. 76091
   c. 76092
   d. 76092-50

8. A 75-year-old patient is followed in the nursing home for residual hemiplegia of the dominant side after a cerebrovascular accident three years ago. What is the correct ICD-9-CM code to report to Medicare?
   a. 434.91
   b. 436
   c. 438.21
   d. V12.59

9. A 58-year-old male complaining of chest pain has an electrocardiogram done in the office. The EKG is abnormal showing nonspecific ST segment changes in leads V–VII. Further outpatient testing will be scheduled to rule out any cardiac disorders or abnormalities. How would this be correctly coded for reimbursement?
   a. Cardiac disorder, etiology undetermined
   b. Chest pain with abnormal EKG
   c. Noncardiac chest pain
   d. Probable myocardial infarction

10. What is the purpose of providing an insurance carrier with ICD-9-CM and CPT codes correctly linked to the patient's care?
   a. To complete the advance beneficiary notice
   b. To document the patient has medical insurance
   c. To provide for coordination of benefits
   d. To show the medical necessity for services and procedures performed

REVIEW QUESTIONS

1. Review the patient information form in the textbook. Answer the following questions.
   a. What is the purpose of requesting home, work, and/or cell phone numbers?
   _____

   b. Why is the name and contact information of an emergency contact important?
   _____

   c. What should be done in addition to requesting insurance information on the form?
   _____

   d. Why would you question a condition related to an accident? _____
   _____

   e. How does the referral information relate to submitting an insurance claim?
   _____

2. An 8-year-old patient is scheduled for a tonsillectomy to be performed in the ambulatory surgical center. The patient has no insurance coverage and the parents arrange a payment plan with the surgeon's office with payments to be made monthly for six months. What financial form is completed for this procedure?

   a. Advance beneficiary notice

   b. HIPAA confidentiality form

   c. Surgical consent form

   d. Truth-in-lending agreement

3. Place an "x" in the space provided to indicate information to include on a patient statement.

   _____ Patient's name and address

   _____ Patient's date of birth/age

   _____ Date of service/procedure

   _____ Description of service/procedure

   _____ Patient's next-of-kin

   _____ Patient's telephone number

   _____ Provider's name, address, telephone number

   _____ Patient's chief complaint for service/procedure

   _____ Patient's social security number

   _____ Charges, payments, adjustments

4. The purpose of the Fair Debt Collection Practices Act is to protect consumers against abusive practices by debt collectors. In the space provided, put "T" for each statement that is true, "F" for each statement that is false as it relates to this act.

   _____ Cannot threaten to notify an employer that a consumer has not paid bills.

   _____ Calls are to be made between 8 a.m. and 9 p.m.

   _____ The time difference in a region does not matter when calling for debt collection purposes.

   _____ Embarrassing a consumer by advertising or publishing debt information is acceptable.

   _____ A special collection fee can be added to the amount that is owed.

5. Place an "x" in the space provided to indicate correct procedure for billing for a deceased patient.

   _____ Address statement to the deceased at last known address.

   _____ Address the statement to the estate of (patient's name) mailed to last known address.

   _____ Accept assignment when billing third-party payer.

   _____ Send the statement as soon as the patient expires.

   _____ Contact probate court to check status of estate/will.

Chapter 14
Filing the Claim Form

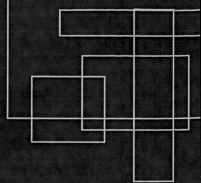

Understanding the concept of health insurance and how to complete the claim form for submission to the insurance carrier is an important part of the billing process whether it is electronic claim filing or a traditional CMS-1500 claim form. The initial contact at the reception desk of a medical practice or patient registration at other facilities begins the process of obtaining correct demographic and insurance information that will allow coders and billers to abstract chart notes to submit claims to a third-party payer. In addition, understanding the reason for rejection or denial of a submitted claim assists in the resubmission of the claim or in the appeals process to the third-party payer.

A clear understanding of this process results in accurate claims with correct payment to the provider. The insurance specialist will also be familiar with the various third party payers and their individual requirements for claim submission and reimbursement. This includes knowing the status of participating versus nonparticipating providers, and the medical necessity for services rendered, both in the office or outpatient setting and the inpatient facility.

Coding Review

To answer the following questions, refer to the CMS-1500 form shown.

1. A primary care physician refers a patient for outpatient physical therapy following a fracture of the tibia and fibula. What blocks of the CMS-1500 are required to designate a referring physician when the claim is filed by the physical therapy provider?

    a. 15 and 16

    b. 17 and 17a

    c. 24D and E

    d. 32 and 33

2. A patient is admitted to the hospital by the primary care physician for pneumonia on April 5. The PCP sees the patient daily on April 6, 7, and 8, then discharges the patient on April 9. The following days in the hospital are billed the same level of CPT. What will be entered in Block 24G of the CMS-1500?

    a. 2

    b. 3

    c. 4

    d. 5

PLEASE
DO NOT
STAPLE
IN THIS
AREA

CARRIER

HEALTH INSURANCE CLAIM FORM

| | PICA | | | | | | | | | PICA | |

1. MEDICARE   MEDICAID   CHAMPUS   CHAMPVA   GROUP HEALTH PLAN   FECA BLK LUNG   OTHER   1a. INSURED'S I.D. NUMBER   (FOR PROGRAM IN ITEM 1)

(Medicare #)   (Medicaid #)   (Sponsor's SSN)   (VA File #)   (SSN or ID)   (SSN)   (ID)

2. PATIENT'S NAME (Last Name, First Name, Middle Initial)

3. PATIENT'S BIRTH DATE   MM   DD   YY   SEX   M   F

4. INSURED'S NAME (Last Name, First Name, Middle Initial)

5. PATIENT'S ADDRESS (No., Street)

6. PATIENT RELATIONSHIP TO INSURED   Self   Spouse   Child   Other

7. INSURED'S ADDRESS (No., Street)

CITY   STATE

8. PATIENT STATUS   Single   Married   Other

CITY   STATE

ZIP CODE   TELEPHONE (Include Area Code)   (   )

Employed   Full-Time Student   Part-Time Student

ZIP CODE   TELEPHONE (INCLUDE AREA CODE)   (   )

9. OTHER INSURED'S NAME (Last Name, First Name, Middle Initial)

10. IS PATIENT'S CONDITION RELATED TO:

11. INSURED'S POLICY GROUP OR FECA NUMBER

a. OTHER INSURED'S POLICY OR GROUP NUMBER

a. EMPLOYMENT? (CURRENT OR PREVIOUS)   YES   NO

a. INSURED'S DATE OF BIRTH   MM   DD   YY   SEX   M   F

b. OTHER INSURED'S DATE OF BIRTH   MM   DD   YY   SEX   M   F

b. AUTO ACCIDENT?   PLACE (State)   YES   NO

b. EMPLOYER'S NAME OR SCHOOL NAME

c. EMPLOYER'S NAME OR SCHOOL NAME

c. OTHER ACCIDENT?   YES   NO

c. INSURANCE PLAN NAME OR PROGRAM NAME

d. INSURANCE PLAN NAME OR PROGRAM NAME

10d. RESERVED FOR LOCAL USE

d. IS THERE ANOTHER HEALTH BENEFIT PLAN?   YES   NO   If yes, return to and complete item 9 a-d.

READ BACK OF FORM BEFORE COMPLETING & SIGNING THIS FORM.
12. PATIENT'S OR AUTHORIZED PERSON'S SIGNATURE I authorize the release of any medical or other information necessary to process this claim. I also request payment of government benefits either to myself or to the party who accepts assignment below.

SIGNED _____   DATE _____

13. INSURED'S OR AUTHORIZED PERSON'S SIGNATURE I authorize payment of medical benefits to the undersigned physician or supplier for services described below.

SIGNED _____

14. DATE OF CURRENT: ILLNESS (First symptom) OR INJURY (Accident) OR PREGNANCY(LMP)   MM   DD   YY

15. IF PATIENT HAS HAD SAME OR SIMILAR ILLNESS. GIVE FIRST DATE   MM   DD   YY

16. DATES PATIENT UNABLE TO WORK IN CURRENT OCCUPATION   MM   DD   YY   FROM   TO   MM   DD   YY

17. NAME OF REFERRING PHYSICIAN OR OTHER SOURCE

17a. I.D. NUMBER OF REFERRING PHYSICIAN

18. HOSPITALIZATION DATES RELATED TO CURRENT SERVICES   MM   DD   YY   FROM   TO   MM   DD   YY

19. RESERVED FOR LOCAL USE

20. OUTSIDE LAB?   YES   NO $ CHARGES

21. DIAGNOSIS OR NATURE OF ILLNESS OR INJURY. (RELATE ITEMS 1,2,3 OR 4 TO ITEM 24E BY LINE)

1. |___.___   3. |___.___

2. |___.___   4. |___.___

22. MEDICAID RESUBMISSION CODE   ORIGINAL REF. NO.

23. PRIOR AUTHORIZATION NUMBER

24. A						B	C	D		E	F	G	H	I	J	K
DATE(S) OF SERVICE						Place of Service	Type of Service	PROCEDURES, SERVICES, OR SUPPLIES (Explain Unusual Circumstances)		DIAGNOSIS CODE	$ CHARGES	DAYS OR UNITS	EPSDT Family Plan	EMG	COB	RESERVED FOR LOCAL USE
From			To					CPT/HCPCS	MODIFIER							
MM	DD	YY	MM	DD	YY											
1																
2																
3																
4																
5																
6																

25. FEDERAL TAX I.D. NUMBER   SSN   EIN

26. PATIENT'S ACCOUNT NO.

27. ACCEPT ASSIGNMENT? (For govt. claims, see back)   YES   NO

28. TOTAL CHARGE $

29. AMOUNT PAID $

30. BALANCE DUE $

31. SIGNATURE OF PHYSICIAN OR SUPPLIER INCLUDING DEGREES OR CREDENTIALS (I certify that the statements on the reverse apply to this bill and are made a part thereof.)

SIGNED _____   DATE _____

32. NAME AND ADDRESS OF FACILITY WHERE SERVICES WERE RENDERED (If other than home or office)

33. PHYSICIAN'S, SUPPLIER'S BILLING NAME, ADDRESS, ZIP CODE & PHONE #

PIN#   GRP#

(APPROVED BY AMA COUNCIL ON MEDICAL SERVICE 8/88)   **PLEASE PRINT OR TYPE**   APPROVED OMB-0938-0008 FORM CMS-1500 (12/90),   FORM RRB-1500
APPROVED OMB-1215-0055 FORM OWCP-1500, APPROVED OMB-0720-0001 (CHAMPUS)

PATIENT AND INSURED INFORMATION

PHYSICIAN OR SUPPLIER INFORMATION

3. A patient is seen in the office for an eye injury sustained at work when a piece of metal he was welding went into his right eye. What block of the CMS-1500 must be marked to indicate a work-related injury?

   a. 10a

   b. 10b

   c. 10c

   d. 10d

4. A physician makes monthly rounds at a nursing home that provides skilled nursing services to its residents. What is the POS code required in 24B of the CMS-1500?

   a. 13

   b. 31

   c. 32

   d. 33

5. A retired patient has Medicare that is primary and an Aetna supplemental policy with his former employer. What block of the CMS-1500 is required for Medicare to cross over the claim to Aetna?

   a. 1a

   b. 9a-d

   c. 10a-c

   d. 11a-c

6. What is missing from the following CMS-1500 form that would reject the claim?

_____

1. MEDICARE MEDICAID CHAMPUS CHAMPVA GROUP HEALTH PLAN FECA BLK LUNG OTHER	1a. INSURED'S I.D. NUMBER (FOR PROGRAM IN ITEM 1)
☒ (Medicare #) ☐ (Medicaid #) ☐ (Sponsor's SSN) ☐ (VA File #) ☐ (SSN or ID) ☐ (SSN) ☐ (ID)	
2. PATIENT'S NAME (Last Name, First Name, Middle Initial) Smith, James, B	3. PATIENT'S BIRTH DATE MM 01 DD 05 YY SEX M ☒ F ☐	4. INSURED'S NAME (Last Name, First Name, Middle Initial) same as patient

5. PATIENT'S ADDRESS (No., Street) 206 Short St	6. PATIENT RELATIONSHIP TO INSURED Self ☒ Spouse ☐ Child ☐ Other ☐	7. INSURED'S ADDRESS (No., Street) same as patient
CITY Millville STATE OH	8. PATIENT STATUS Single ☐ Married ☒ Other ☐	CITY STATE
ZIP CODE 12345 TELEPHONE (Include Area Code) ( )	Employed ☐ Full-Time Student ☐ Part-Time Student ☐	ZIP CODE TELEPHONE (INCLUDE AREA CODE) ( )
9. OTHER INSURED'S NAME (Last Name, First Name, Middle Initial)	10. IS PATIENT'S CONDITION RELATED TO:	11. INSURED'S POLICY GROUP OR FECA NUMBER
a. OTHER INSURED'S POLICY OR GROUP NUMBER	a. EMPLOYMENT? (CURRENT OR PREVIOUS) ☐ YES ☒ NO	a. INSURED'S DATE OF BIRTH MM DD YY SEX M ☐ F ☐
b. OTHER INSURED'S DATE OF BIRTH MM DD YY SEX M ☐ F ☐	b. AUTO ACCIDENT? PLACE (State) ☐ YES ☒ NO	b. EMPLOYER'S NAME OR SCHOOL NAME
c. EMPLOYER'S NAME OR SCHOOL NAME	c. OTHER ACCIDENT? ☐ YES ☒ NO	c. INSURANCE PLAN NAME OR PROGRAM NAME
d. INSURANCE PLAN NAME OR PROGRAM NAME	10d. RESERVED FOR LOCAL USE	d. IS THERE ANOTHER HEALTH BENEFIT PLAN? ☐ YES ☒ NO If yes, return to and complete item 9 a-d.

7. A patient has a blepharoplasty of both upper eyelids performed by a well-known plastic surgeon. What is the coding error on the following CMS-1500 form that would result in lower payment of the procedure? _____

21. DIAGNOSIS OR NATURE OF ILLNESS OR INJURY. (RELATE ITEMS 1,2,3 OR 4 TO ITEM 24E BY LINE)					22. MEDICAID RESUBMISSION CODE ORIGINAL REF. NO.					
1. L 374 . 30		3. L___ . __			23. PRIOR AUTHORIZATION NUMBER					
2. L___ . __		4. L___ . __								

24. A DATE(S) OF SERVICE From · To MM DD YY · MM DD YY	B Place of Service	C Type of Service	D PROCEDURES, SERVICES, OR SUPPLIES (Explain Unusual Circumstances) CPT/HCPCS | MODIFIER	E DIAGNOSIS CODE	F $ CHARGES	G DAYS OR UNITS	H EPSDT Family Plan	I EMG	J COB	K RESERVED FOR LOCAL USE
1			15822 |		850 ¦ 00					
2										
3										
4										
5										
6										

8. A patient is referred by Dr. Dogood to Dr. Bones, an orthopedic surgeon, for evaluation of pain in the left knee joint. An x-ray of the left knee reveals a torn medial meniscus. A CMS-1500 form is completed by Dr. Bones's office for the office visit and x-ray of the left knee to the insurance company. What is missing on the following CMS-1500 form? _____

14. DATE OF CURRENT: ILLNESS (First symptom) OR MM ¦ DD ¦ YY INJURY (Accident) OR PREGNANCY(LMP)	15. IF PATIENT HAS HAD SAME OR SIMILAR ILLNESS. GIVE FIRST DATE MM ¦ DD ¦ YY	16. DATES PATIENT UNABLE TO WORK IN CURRENT OCCUPATION MM ¦ DD ¦ YY MM ¦ DD ¦ YY FROM TO
17. NAME OF REFERRING PHYSICIAN OR OTHER SOURCE	17a. I.D. NUMBER OF REFERRING PHYSICIAN	18. HOSPITALIZATION DATES RELATED TO CURRENT SERVICES MM ¦ DD ¦ YY MM ¦ DD ¦ YY FROM TO
19. RESERVED FOR LOCAL USE		20. OUTSIDE LAB? $ CHARGES ☐ YES ☐ NO

21. DIAGNOSIS OR NATURE OF ILLNESS OR INJURY. (RELATE ITEMS 1,2,3 OR 4 TO ITEM 24E BY LINE)					22. MEDICAID RESUBMISSION CODE ORIGINAL REF. NO.					
1. L 836 . 0		3. L___ . __			23. PRIOR AUTHORIZATION NUMBER					
2. L___ . __		4. L___ . __								

24. A DATE(S) OF SERVICE From · To MM DD YY · MM DD YY	B Place of Service	C Type of Service	D PROCEDURES, SERVICES, OR SUPPLIES (Explain Unusual Circumstances) CPT/HCPCS | MODIFIER	E DIAGNOSIS CODE	F $ CHARGES	G DAYS OR UNITS	H EPSDT Family Plan	I EMG	J COB	K RESERVED FOR LOCAL USE
1	11		99205 |	1	95 ¦ 00	1				
2	11		73560 | LT	1	75 ¦ 00	1				
3										
4										
5										
6										

9. A patient diagnosed with anemia is sent to the lab for a CBC with differential, iron and iron binding capacity, and a stool for occult blood. What is the coding error submitted on the following CMS-1500 form? _____

21. DIAGNOSIS OR NATURE OF ILLNESS OR INJURY. (RELATE ITEMS 1,2,3 OR 4 TO ITEM 24E BY LINE)								22. MEDICAID RESUBMISSION CODE ORIGINAL REF. NO.					
1. 258.9 3. ___.___								23. PRIOR AUTHORIZATION NUMBER					
2. ___.___ 4. ___.___													

24. A DATE(S) OF SERVICE						B Place of Service	C Type of Service	D PROCEDURES, SERVICES, OR SUPPLIES (Explain Unusual Circumstances) CPT/HCPCS | MODIFIER	E DIAGNOSIS CODE	F $ CHARGES	G DAYS OR UNITS	H EPSDT Family Plan	I EMG	J COB	K RESERVED FOR LOCAL USE
MM	DD	YY	MM	DD	YY										
1								85025							
2								83540							
3								83550							
4								82270							
5															
6															

10. A patient is seen in the office complaining of rectal burning and discomfort, especially with bowel movements. Examination today reveals a perianal abscess. This is incised and drained and the patient will return in five days for recheck. What is the coding error on the CMS-1500 form below?

_____

21. DIAGNOSIS OR NATURE OF ILLNESS OR INJURY. (RELATE ITEMS 1,2,3 OR 4 TO ITEM 24E BY LINE)								22. MEDICAID RESUBMISSION CODE ORIGINAL REF. NO.					
1. 682.2 3. ___.___								23. PRIOR AUTHORIZATION NUMBER					
2. ___.___ 4. ___.___													

24. A DATE(S) OF SERVICE						B Place of Service	C Type of Service	D PROCEDURES, SERVICES, OR SUPPLIES (Explain Unusual Circumstances) CPT/HCPCS | MODIFIER	E DIAGNOSIS CODE	F $ CHARGES	G DAYS OR UNITS	H EPSDT Family Plan	I EMG	J COB	K RESERVED FOR LOCAL USE
MM	DD	YY	MM	DD	YY										
1								46050	1						
2															
3															
4															
5															
6															

CASE STUDIES

In Case Studies 1–7, complete a CMS-1500 claim form for each patient's insurance plan as indicated in the patient information. Blank CMS-1500 forms are provided at the end of this workbook.

Provider Billing Information

Physician:	Dalton Dogood, M.D.
	Internal Medicine
Address:	2222 Oldenburg St.
	Newtown, PA 12345
Phone:	(222) 777-1515
Employer ID No. 65-2233456	
PIN:	2525

Participates with Medicare, Medicaid, and most insurance plans.

Hospital services performed at: Getwell Community Hospital
8567 Tremor Rd.
Newtown, PA 12345

Case Study 1

Patient Information

Name:	Susie Jacuzzi
Address:	2551 Maker St., Apt. 1
	Newtown, PA 12345
Phone:	(222) 774-2987
Date of Birth:	02/25/1995
Occupation:	Student
Employer:	N/A
Gender:	Female
Marital Status:	Single

Insurance Information

Primary Insurance: United Health Care

ID No.: 4122907233

Group No.: 78900

Policyholder: Jack Jacuzzi

Policyholder DOB: 11/04/1961

Employer: GWC Corporation

Relationship to Insured: Child

Secondary Insurance:

Policyholder:

Policyholder DOB:

ID No.:

Group No.:

Employer:

Relationship to Patient:

Chart Notes

Patient: Susie Jacuzzi

Date: 06/15/20XX

This is a new patient seen in the office today for a rash of her lower extremities. She states she went hiking yesterday and noticed the rash with itching after she took a shower last night. She has used cortisone cream that she had at home to try to relieve the itching but her symptoms have continued. She is given an injection of Decadron-LA 1 mg. IM right deltoid, and a prescription for Decadron-LA p.o.

If the rash does not clear with the medication, she will be referred to a dermatologist.

Diagnosis: Rash of unknown etiology

Dalton Dogood, M.D.

Account Information

Date	Procedure or Service	Charge
6/15/20XX	Office Visit, PF	$65.00
6/15/20XX	IM injection Decadron-LA 1 mg.	$10.00
	Decadron-LA 1 mg.	$18.00

Case Study 2

Patient Information

Name:	Don Swan
Address:	106 Canal St.
	Newtown, PA 12345
Phone:	(222) 788-2322
Date of Birth:	03/03/1933
Occupation:	Retired firefighter
Employer:	Retired, Newtown FD
Gender:	Male
Marital Status:	Married

Insurance Information

Primary Insurance: Medicare

ID No.: 402229380A

Group No.:

Policyholder: Self

Policyholder DOB:

Employer:

Relationship to Insured: Self

Secondary Insurance: Mutual of Omaha

Policyholder: Self

Policyholder DOB:

ID No.: 402229380

Group No.: 610

Employer: Retired, Newtown FD

Relationship to Patient: Self

Chart Notes

Patient: Don Swan

Date: 01/10/20XX

Mr. Swan is seen in the office today for recheck of his blood pressure and antihypertensive medications. As noted last month, his B/P was 188/98. At that visit he was started on Norvasc 5 mg. in an attempt to lower the blood pressure.

Vitals today: B/P is 142/82. Weight 196 1/2 lbs. Pulse 76 and regular. Respirations 18.

His chest and lungs are clear. Heart rate NSR. He states he feels good and has had no problems with the medication. He will continue the Norvasc 5 mg. one each morning. To return two months for recheck of his blood pressure.

Diagnosis: Benign hypertension

Dalton Dogood, M.D.

Account Information

Date	Procedure or Service	Charge
1/10/20XX	Office Visit, EPF	$58.00

Case Study 3

Patient Information

Name:	Angela S. Smyth
Address:	2012 N. 5th St.
	Weston, PA 12356
Phone:	None
Date of Birth:	10/30/1975
Occupation:	Unemployed
Employer:	
Gender:	Female
Marital Status:	Divorced

Insurance Information

Primary Insurance: Medicaid

ID No.: 112612789003

Group No.:

Policyholder: Self

Policyholder DOB:

Employer:

Relationship to Insured:

Secondary Insurance:

Policyholder:

Policyholder DOB:

ID No.:

Group No.:

Employer:

Relationship to Patient:

Chart Notes

Patient: Angela M. Smyth

Date: 07/01/20XX

This is a former patient returning to this office after living out of town the past five years. She has non-insulin dependent diabetes. She also states she has been having frequent migraine headaches. She has been on Imitrex in the past for the migraines. She is in today for evaluation of her diabetes and her headaches.

Examination today: B/P is 118/68. Weight 165 lbs. Chest and lungs are clear. Heart is normal. She states her blood sugar levels checked at home have been normal. HEENT normal.

Blood is drawn in the office today for a quantitative glucose to be sent to the lab. She is given a new prescription for the Imitrex 50 mg. and Glucophage 500 mg. She will continue to check her glucose at home and report levels to this office. She will return for recheck in three months.

Diagnosis:

1. Diabetes mellitus, noninsulin dependent

2. Migraine headaches

Dalton Dogood, M.D.

Account Information

Date	Procedure or Service	Charge
7/01/20XX	Office Visit, detailed	$65.00
7/01/20XX	Venipuncture	$10.00

Case Study 4

Patient Information

Name:	Thomas Thom
Address:	678 Wildwood Ave.
	Oldtown, PA 12359
Phone:	(222) 642-2270
Date of Birth:	08/11/1928
Occupation:	Disabled
Employer:	
Gender:	Male
Marital Status:	Widowed

Insurance Information

Primary Insurance: Medicare

ID No.: 212778989W1

Group No.:

Policyholder: Self

Policyholder DOB:

Employer:

Relationship to Insured:

Secondary Insurance: Medicaid

Policyholder: Self

Policyholder DOB:

ID No.: 10004304021

Group No.:

Employer:

Relationship to Patient:

Chart Notes

Patient: Thomas Thom

Date: 06/28/20XX

Patient called to state he was having difficulty breathing, especially when lying down. Just generally overall felt weak and shaky. He is admitted to the hospital as a direct admission.

Discharged from hospital 07/03/20XX to his home. He will be seen in my office in one week.

See hospital admission H & P and Discharge summary for treatment/meds.

Diagnosis: 1. Chronic obstructive asthma

                     2. Bronchial pneumonia

Dalton Dogood, M.D.

Account Information

Date	Procedure or Service	Charge
6/28/20XX	Hospital admission, detailed, low comp.	$175.00
6/29/20XX	Hospital care follow, EPF, mod. comp.	$85.00
6/30/20XX	Hospital care follow, EPF, mod. comp.	$85.00
7/1/20XX	Hospital care follow, EPF, mod. comp.	$85.00
7/2/20XX	Hospital care follow, PF, mod. comp.	$75.00
7/3/20XX	Discharge, 45 min.	$75.00

Case Study 5

Patient Information

Name:	William J. Suey
Address:	2515 Best Rd.
	Weston, PA 12356
Phone:	(222) 807-9331
Date of Birth:	09/05/1954
Occupation:	Painter
Employer:	Brothers' Painters
Gender:	Male
Marital Status:	Married

Insurance Information

Primary Insurance: BC/BS

ID No.: MR2500673109

Group No.: 20553

Policyholder: Self

Policyholder DOB:

Employer: Brothers' Painters

Relationship to Insured: Self

Secondary Insurance:

Policyholder: Self

Policyholder DOB:

ID No.:

Group No.:

Employer:

Relationship to Patient:

Chart Notes

Patient: William J. Suey

Date: 02/02/20XX

Scheduled for routine physical exam. He is a new patient in the practice. Examination today reveals a nodule in the areola of the left breast. There is some discomfort with palpation but no real pain. No other symptoms. The patient is scheduled for an ultrasound of the breast. The exam today includes a detailed history and examination with medical decision making of moderate complexity. He will return after the ultrasound.

Diagnosis: Nodule in the areola of left breast, R/O carcinoma

Dalton Dogood, M.D.

Account Information

Date	Procedure or Service	Charge
2/2/20XX	Routine physical exam	$115.00
2/2/20XX	Office visit, detailed/mod. comp.	$85.00

Case Study 6

Patient Information

Name:	Donna A. Dean
Address:	2103 Morris Way
	Oldtown, PA 12359
Phone:	(222) 642-8090
Date of Birth:	12/30/1980
Occupation:	Cashier
Employer:	Dolan's Dept. Store
Gender:	Female
Marital Status:	Married

Insurance Information

Primary Insurance: Cigna

ID No.: 333176694R10

Group No.: 30333

Policyholder: Donald B. Dean

Policyholder DOB: 07/14/1978

Employer: JAR Auto Mart

Relationship to Insured: Spouse

Secondary Insurance:

Policyholder:

Policyholder DOB:

ID No.:

Group No.:

Employer:

Relationship to Patient:

Chart Notes

Patient: Donna A. Dean

Date: 04/01/20XX

This established patient is seen today for routine yearly pelvic exam with Pap smear. She and her husband have decided they are ready to have another child and will discontinue present contraceptive measures. B/P today is 112/78. Weight 124 lbs. She states she has no complaints today. No abnormalities are indicated in the course of this examination. Urinalysis done today in the office is normal. She will be called when the results of the Pap smear are received.

Diagnosis: Routine annual pelvic examination

Dalton Dogood, M.D.

Account Information

Date	Procedure or Service	Charge
4/1/20XX	Annual pelvic examination w/Pap smear	$135.00
4/1/20XX	Urinalysis, dipstick	$12.00

Case Study 7

Patient Information

Name:	Mayme B. Brown
Address:	6711 Bumble Bee Ln.
	Weston, PA 12356
Phone:	(222) 807-3340
Date of Birth:	10/02/1929
Occupation:	Homemaker
Employer:	
Gender:	Female
Marital Status:	Married

Insurance Information

Primary Insurance: Medicare

ID No.: 301012245B

Group No.:

Policyholder: Self

Policyholder DOB:

Employer:

Relationship to Insured:

Secondary Insurance: AARP

Policyholder: Aaron D. Brown

Policyholder DOB: 05/09/1928

ID No.: 33329057710

Group No.: 2550

Employer: Self-employed

Relationship to Patient: Spouse

Chart Notes

Patient: Mayme Brown

Date: 02/25/20XX

This patient is referred to this office by Dr. Henry McHenry, with the complaint of her legs feeling "twitchy," with a burning sensation that keeps her awake most of the night. She usually has to get out of bed to walk when this occurs, which really does not relieve her symptoms. She states she has these symptoms at least four nights each week.

A detailed history and examination reveals she may have restless leg syndrome. It is explained to her this diagnosis is based on her symptoms; there is no x-ray or blood test to diagnose RLS. Her medical history reveals she is being treated by Dr. McHenry for hypothyroidism. It is explained to her that restless leg syndrome can be related to hypothyroidism, and she should continue the Synthroid prescribed by Dr. McHenry.

The patient is given a prescription today for Neurontin as a trial for RLS. She will return here in one month for follow-up of her symptoms and the medication.

Diagnosis: Restless leg syndrome

Dalton Dogood, M.D.

Follow-up: 03/04/20XX

Patient returns today for follow-up. She has taken the Neurontin for one month and states her symptoms are much improved with the medication. She will remain on the Neurontin and be followed for this condition by Dr. McHenry, her PCP.

Dalton Dogood, M.D.

Account Information

Date	Procedure or Service	Charge
2/25/20XX	Office consultation, detailed	$210.00
3/4/20XX	Office visit, follow-up, PF	$65.00

In Case Studies 8–10, complete a CMS-1500 claim form for each patient's insurance plan as indicated in the patient information. Blank CMS-1500 forms are provided at the end of this workbook.

Provider Billing Information

Physician: Kenneth Sharpknife, M.D.

                    General Surgery

Address: 8570 Tremor Rd.

                    Newtown, PA 12345

Phone: (222) 777-5600

Employer ID No. 55-9099238

PIN: 1011

Participates with Medicare, Medicaid, and most insurance plans.

Hospital services performed at: Getwell Community Hospital

                                                  8567 Tremor Rd.

                                                  Newtown, PA 12345

Case Study 8

Patient Information

Name:	Connie Y. Davidson
Address:	7318 Country Mile Ln.
	Newtown, PA 12345
Phone:	(222) 778-9241
Date of Birth:	01/31/1965
Occupation:	Administrative Assistant
Employer:	Wells Fargo Bank
Gender:	Female
Marital Status:	Married

Insurance Information

Primary Insurance: Metropolitan

ID No.: YMM501243389

Group No.: 5000

Policyholder: Self

Policyholder DOB:

Employer:

Relationship to Insured: Self

Secondary Insurance: BC-BS

Policyholder: Brad R. Davidson

Policyholder DOB: 08/09/1961

ID No.: 333905022

Group No.: 20502

Employer: Driskell Pharmaceuticals

Relationship to Patient: Spouse

Chart Notes

Patient: Connie Davidson

Date: 07/25/20XX

Patient was brought into the Getwell Community Hospital Emergency Department with severe right-sided pain radiating to the LUQ. It began early this morning and has increased in severity throughout the day and into the night. She has nausea with vomiting and states she feels feverish with chills.

Examination reveals extreme pain and tenderness all over the abdomen, particularly in both right lower and upper quadrants. Temp. is 100.2. WBC is elevated at 18,000. CT scan of the abdomen reveals a ruptured appendix with generalized peritonitis.

In addition, she is hypertensive with a B/P in the ED of 208/104. She states she did not take her antihypertensive medication today due to being so ill.

She is taken to the OR for appendectomy performed by this surgeon. Her PCP, Dr. McHenry, is called in to treat the hypertension.

Impression: Ruptured appendix with generalized peritonitis

Kenneth Sharpknife, M.D.

Account Information

Date	Procedure or Service	Charge
7/25/20XX	Appendectomy	$1200.00
8/16/20XX	Ins. Pymt. Rec'd	-$640.00

For Case Study 9, file a claim for the balance remaining with the patient's secondary insurance policy. Blank CMS-1500 forms are provided at the end of this workbook.

Case Study 9

Patient Information

Name:	Tony Tigger
Address:	610 Tiger Rd.
	Oldtown, PA 12359
Phone:	(222) 595-1034
Date of Birth:	02/14/1998
Occupation:	Student
Employer:	
Gender:	Male
Marital Status:	Single

Insurance Information

Primary Insurance: Medicaid

ID No.: 22160110103

Group No.:

Policyholder: Self

Policyholder DOB:

Employer:

Relationship to Insured:

Secondary Insurance:

Policyholder:

Policyholder DOB:

ID No.:

Group No.:

Employer:

Relationship to Patient:

Chart Notes

Patient: Tony Tigger

Date: 04/25/20XX

This young patient is referred by Dr. Dogood for outpatient tonsillectomy and adenoidectomy. His mother states he has had chronic tonsillitis since age 3. He was recently treated by Dr. Dogood for a severe sore throat. The tonsils continue to be enlarged and inflamed.

Preauthorization number for this outpatient procedure issued by Medicaid is 891026347.

Diagnosis: Recurrent chronic tonsillitis

Kenneth Sharpknife, M.D.

Account Information

Date	Procedure or Service	Charge
4/25/20XX	Tonsillectomy and adenoidectomy	$1050.00
5/30/20XX	Medicaid Pymt. Rec'd	-$326.50

Refer to the previous account information. The procedure is an allowed service by Medicaid. What must be done with the balance remaining after the Medicaid payment is received in the office? _____

Case Study 10

Patient Information

Name:	William J. Suey
Address:	2515 Best Rd.
	Weston, PA 12356
Phone:	(222) 807-9331
Date of Birth:	09/05/1954
Occupation:	Painter
Employer:	Brothers' Painters
Gender:	Male
Marital Status:	Married

Insurance Information

Primary Insurance: BC/BS

ID No.: MR2500673109

Group No.: 20553

Policyholder: Self

Policyholder DOB:

Employer: Brothers' Painters

Relationship to Insured: Self

Secondary Insurance:

Policyholder:

ID No.:

Group No.:

Employer:

Relationship to Patient:

Chart Notes

Patient: William J. Suey

Date: 02/20/20XX

Patient referred by Dr. Dogood following an ultrasound of the left breast that revealed a tumor in the areola. A biopsy revealed carcinoma of the areola of the breast. He is admitted to the hospital for a radical mastectomy of the left breast.

Diagnosis: Carcinoma of the areola of the left breast

Kenneth Sharpknife, M.D.

Account Information

Date	Procedure or Service	Charge
2/20/20XX	Radical mastectomy, left breast	$1125.00
2/21/20XX	Hospital follow visit	
2/21/20XX	Hospital discharge, 20 minutes	

REVIEW QUESTIONS

1. Which one of the following is *not* true of Medicaid?
   a. It is a medical assistance program for medically indigent low-income persons.
   b. It covers aged and disabled persons on SSI or QMB.
   c. It covers persons in institutional or long-term care facilities.
   d. It always serves as the primary carrier for medical coverage.

2. Which one of the following is *not* eligible for Medicare benefits?
   a. A 68-year-old male, retired, receiving Social Security benefits
   b. A 55-year-old male receiving Social Security Disability Insurance benefits for four years
   c. An 18-year-old pregnant female with gestational hypertension and diabetes
   d. A 72-year-old widow whose husband retired from the federal government

3. Which one of the following may be considered medically unnecessary by Medicare?
   a. Application of short leg walking cast
   b. Experimental chemotherapy treatment for colon cancer
   c. Holter monitor to document and assess premature ventricular contractions
   d. Immunization for influenza and pneumonia

4. When would a Medicare claim be filed as secondary coverage?
   a. A 45-year-old disabled patient receiving SSDI benefits
   b. A 66-year-old patient working full-time
   c. A 72-year-old patient in a skilled nursing facility
   d. An 80-year-old patient receiving Medicaid benefits

5. What does the term "sponsor" mean for TRICARE/CHAMPVA patients?
   a. The insurance plan or program name
   b. The insured or subscriber, whether active duty, retired, or deceased
   c. The provider of the medical service or treatment
   d. The referring physician/facility

6. What is the largest single medical program in the United States offering benefits in all 50 states?
   a. Blue Cross/Blue Shield
   b. Medicaid
   c. Medicare
   d. TRICARE

7. A patient is treated in the emergency department for a back injury after falling from a ladder in the storage facility in the plant where he works. He complained of dizziness prior to the fall, and his blood pressure today is elevated. His employer requests the worker's medical records from his primary care physician to determine if there is a history of hypertension or previous problems with blood pressure that may be related to the fall. A medical clerk faxes the requested information to the employer without the patient's authorization. What defines this breach of confidentiality?

a. AFL-CIO

b. CMS

c. HIPAA

d. Workers' Compensation law

8. A patient is seen in the surgeon's office four weeks following an open cholecystectomy. The patient has done well with no complaints and is released to normal activities, including returning to work. How is the office visit coded?

a. A follow-up office consultation

b. A new patient office visit

c. An established patient office visit

d. Included in the global surgical fee package

9. Which one of the following is *not* a nonphysician service?

a. Audiologic testing

b. Durable medical equipment

c. Hospital admission through emergency department

d. Parenteral and enteral nutrition

10. Which one of the following is the computerized database for providers to check eligibility of a TRICARE patient?

a. DEERS

b. HCFA

c. MSDS

d. RBRVS

Chapter 15
Reimbursement, Auditing, and Appeals

Previous chapters have given instruction in correct coding of services and procedures with appropriate linkage of the diagnosis, symptoms, or injury to establish the medical necessity. The importance of medical terminology has been demonstrated to correctly describe the patient's condition, injury, or problem, and accurately describe surgical procedures, diagnostic tests, and other medical services provided. The correct linkage of the diagnosis to the procedures validates the necessity of the physician's work and ensures that services are correctly reported to the insurance company. The result of this process leads to the reimbursement of these procedures and services.

Reimbursement is the action of being paid back or the receipt of remuneration in exchange for goods or services, such as for professional services rendered in the medical office. Reimbursement is received after a request for payment is sent in the form of a statement to the patient, or an insurance claim, such as the CMS-1500, has been submitted. Upcoding, downcoding, and unbundling codes must be avoided as well as understanding what constitutes fraudulent activity. Audits can reveal these activities that can result in refunds of overpayments and financial penalties.

It is important to understand when patients can be billed, and when they cannot be billed. Participation status with Medicare and contracts with other insurers determines what amounts can be billed to and collected from the patient, such as copayments, coinsurance, and deductibles. For example, a laboratory service may be billed for $92.00. Provider contract agreement may determine a payment of $18.00, with an adjustment or write-off of $74.00. The explanation of benefits or remittance summary or advice will address any amount owed to the provider, such as a co-payment. In the example, there is no co-payment required in this plan for laboratory services, so no amount can be billed to the patient.

When errors do occur, corrections must be made. This may be as simple as resubmission of a claim, a telephone call to attempt to correct the problem, or a formal appeal may be requested, which may be a formal letter or completion of a request for appeal or hearing form.

Coding Exercises

Select the appropriate answer from the choices given.

1. A 5-year-old female is seen for routine well-child exam required prior to attending kindergarten. She has been seen in this medical office since birth. She receives the required MMR vaccination. CPT codes submitted are 90707 and 94071. What code is missing, resulting in lower reimbursement of the charges submitted?

    a. 99211

    b. 99212

    c. 99241

    d. 99393

2. An established 52-year-old patient is seen in the office for abdominal pain with projectile vomiting. The exam and history is documented as detailed with moderate complexity decision making. The patient appears ill with the pain worse with palpation to the right lower quadrant of the abdomen. The physician makes arrangements for the patient to be admitted to the hospital directly from the office. How is this coded?

   a. 99214

   b. 99221

   c. 99233

   d. 99253

3. A patient is seen in the office for severe headaches. There is a family history of carcinoma of the brain. An EEG is scheduled as well as an MRI of the brain to rule out a brain tumor. What are the correct ICD-9-CM codes to submit to the insurance company?

   a. 784.0, V16.8, 191.9

   b. 784.0, V16.8

   c. V16.8, 191.9

   d. 784.0, V16.8, 237.5

4. Dr. S performs a total abdominal hysterectomy on a 45-year-old female referred by the hospital emergency department. Dr. T. assists Dr. S. in this procedure. What is the correct code to bill for Dr. T?

   a. 58150

   b. 58150-80

   c. 58200-80

   d. 58263

5. A patient receives an allergy injection weekly in the allergy clinic that has performed the testing and prepared the allergenic extracts. What is (are) the correct code(s) to bill to the patient's insurance company?

   a. 95115

   b. 95120

   c. 95144

   d. 95165

REVIEW QUESTIONS

1. What is the definition of co-payment?

   a. A specified dollar amount paid to the provider for each encounter per contract agreement with the insurance carrier.

   b. A specified percentage paid for medical services after the deductible has been met.

   c. An annual out-of-pocket payment for medical services before payment by a third-party payer.

   d. Payment paid to an insurance carrier for insurance plan coverage.

2. List five reasons a CMS-1500 claim may be rejected based on completion of the form.

   _____

   _____

   _____

_____

_____

3. Which one of the following is not true of the advanced beneficiary notice (ABN)?

    a. Notifies the patient Medicare may not pay for a service it may consider not medically necessary.

    b. The ABN is a written notice given to the patient after the service is rendered.

    c. CPT codes and the total financial obligation for payment must be listed.

    d. A detailed reason must be given as to the reason the claim may be denied.

4. When are new annual ICD-9-CM codes implemented for health insurance plans?

    a. January 1

    b. April 15

    c. October 1

    d. December 31

5. Explain how professional courtesy can be considered a fraudulent activity.

_____

_____

6. An employee in a clinical laboratory reports unbundling of laboratory health panels submitted to Medicaid, resulting in a lawsuit proclaiming this as a fraudulent activity. What is the term for this lawsuit?

    a. Qui tam action

    b. Res ipsa loquitor

    c. Res judicata

    d. Respondent superior

7. What is the division of the DHHS responsible for investigation and enforcement of fraud and abuse cases and legislation?

    a. Health Care Financing Administration

    b. Occupational Health and Safety Administration

    c. Office of the Inspector General

    d. Office of Medicare Hearings and Appeals

8. A patient receives an Explanation of Benefits from his health insurance carrier with the following information:

Date of Service	Billed Charges	Co-Pay Amt.	Payment to Provider
11/21/20XX	$95.00	$15.00	$38.56

What is the amount the provider must adjust per contract agreement? _____

9. A patient receives an Explanation of Benefits from her health insurance company, stating "you are responsible for a charge denied due to medical necessity if you agreed, prior to the service and after seeing the approximate cost in writing, to be responsible for it." What is the name of the notification form to which they are referring?

    a. Advance Beneficiary Notice

    b. Notice of Medical Necessity

    c. Participating Provider Agreement

    d. Redetermination Request Form

10. A patient statement for a colonoscopy with EGD performed by an endoscopy group practice stated the following:

Date of Service	TOS	Charges	Adjustments	Insurance Payment
07/11/20XX	Colonoscopy	1408.00	958.00	375.00
07/11/20XX	EGD	1050.00	1050.00	0.00

What is the amount billed to the patient? _____

11. What is meant by downcoding?
    a. Assignment of a lower-level code than documentation warrants
    b. Reporting multiple codes instead of one specific code that describes the entire service
    c. Selection of a code higher than supported by the documentation
    d. Waiving of co-payment, co-insurance, or deductible

12. Which one of the following is not the correct linkage of a procedure with a diagnosis?
    a. 99203, 81000, 599.0
    b. 84152, 600.00
    c. 99213, 90703, 90471, 034.0
    d. 92002, 367.4

13. Which one of the following contains an error in coding?
    a. ICD-9-CM code 574.60 with CPT 76801
    b. ICD-9-CM code 786.50 with CPT 93000
    c. ICD-9-CM codes 455.1 and 455.4 with CPT 46260
    d. ICD-9-CM code 724.2 with CPT 72132

14. A 26-year-old male is assigned the ICD-9-CM code 642.03 for the CPT code 80055. What is the error in this billing scenario?
    a. Age
    b. Code linkage
    c. Gender
    d. Invalid fifth digit

15. Six weeks later, Dr. S. sees the patient in the office for scheduled follow-up for the hysterectomy. She has done well with no complications and is released to resume normal activities. What is the proper procedure to bill this follow-up visit to her insurance carrier?
    a. It is included in the global surgical package.
    b. It is billed as an established patient office visit.
    c. It is billed as a new patient office visit.
    d. An ABN is signed by the patient as a noncovered service.

16. What blood test would be medically necessary for a patient with a coagulation disorder?
    a. Complete blood count
    b. Occult blood
    c. Potassium
    d. Pro time

17. A physician orders an electrolyte panel. What tests are included in this panel?
    a. CBC, TSH, CO2, potassium
    b. CBC, CO2, potassium, sodium
    c. CO2, chloride, sodium, potassium
    d. Calcium, glucose, potassium, sodium

18. Percutaneous allergy testing includes which of the following?
    a. Patch, prick, puncture
    b. Prick, puncture, scratch
    c. Mantoux, PPD, puncture
    d. Venipuncture, scratch, heel stick

19. In coding for anesthesia, what error is made in the following scenario that would impact reimbursement?

    A 59-year-old male receives general anesthesia for debridement of a second degree burn, 5 percent total body surface. The patient has uncontrolled Type II diabetes. CPT code 01952-P1 is submitted to the insurance company for payment of this procedure.
    a. Incorrect anesthesia code
    b. Incorrect code for total body surface
    c. Incorrect physical status modifier
    d. Absence of a code for qualifying circumstances

20. What coding error is made in the following scenario that would impact reimbursement?
    A 62-year-old female is seen for a nodule in the left breast. A mammogram and ultrasound confirm the nodule, and a biopsy indicates a diagnosis of carcinoma of the left breast. The patient has a simple complete mastectomy. The codes submitted to the insurance company for physician's billing for the mastectomy are 174.9 and 19180-RT.
    a. Incorrect linkage of ICD-9-CM and CPT codes
    b. Incorrect CPT modifier
    c. Incorrect ICD-9-CM code for gender
    d. Nonspecific ICD-9-CM code

Chapter 16
Inpatient Coding

Inpatient coding refers to codes used in acute care or inpatient facilities. Documentation for inpatient hospital coding includes physician documentation, nursing notes and documentation, and ancillary services, such as radiology, laboratory, and physical therapy. Both inpatient coders and outpatient coders follow ICD-9-CM coding guidelines. Volumes 1 and 2 contain codes used for diagnoses and symptoms based on the principal diagnosis established after study for the admission of a patient to the hospital for care. An admission diagnosis is the reason the patient presents to the hospital for treatment. Volume 3 is used for billing in hospitals and skilled nursing facilities with codes for surgical and nonsurgical procedures.

Another difference in outpatient and inpatient billing is the claim or billing form. Hospitals utilize the UB-92 form, while physicians and outpatient facilities utilize the CMS-1500 form to report diagnoses and procedures. In an inpatient setting, conditions identified as "rule out," "probable," or "suspected," documented upon the patient's discharge from the hospital, are coded as if confirmed, unlike the outpatient setting where these conditions cannot be coded.

Coding Exercises

Code the following procedures using Volume 3 of ICD-9-CM.

1. Cholecystectomy _____

2. Esophagogastroduoenoscopy (EGD) _____

3. Suture of laceration of skin of hand _____

4. Laparotomy with herniorrhaphy, bilateral direct inguinal hernia with graft _____

5. Excision, lesion, breast _____

6. Transurethral resection of prostate _____

7. Closed reduction of rt. femur shaft, application skeletal traction _____

8. Needle biopsy of pancreas _____

9. Lt. carotid endarterectomy _____

10. Biopsy lymph node rt. axilla _____

Coding Exercises

Using all three volumes of ICD-9-CM, code the following diagnoses and procedures.

1. Acute cholecystitis with cholelithiasis and
   choledochololithiasis   _____

   Procedure: Laparoscopic cholecystectomy   _____

2. Carcinoma in situ of left breast   _____

   Family hx. of lung cancer   _____

   Procedure: Open biopsy of left breast   _____

3. Uninodular toxic nodular goiter w/thyrotoxicosis   _____

   Procedure: Unilateral thyroid lobectomy   _____

4. Adenocarcinoma left breast w/metastasis to lymph
   nodes of the axilla   _____   _____

   Procedure: Open biopsy of left breast followed by
   radical mastectomy   _____   _____

5. Intractable epilepsy grand mal type   _____

   Procedure: EEG   _____

6. Severe epistaxis due to hypertension   _____ . _____

   Procedure: Nasal packing, anterior   _____

7. Gross, painless hematuria, cause undetermined   _____

   Procedure: IVP   _____

   Procedure: Cystoscopy for control of bladder hemorrhage _____

8. Internal and external thrombosed hemorrhoids   _____   _____

   Procedure: Internal and external hemorrhoidectomy
   by cryosurgery   _____

9. Varicose veins, right leg   _____

   Procedure: Rt. greater saphenous ligation and stripping
   for varicosities   _____

10. Abdominal aortic aneurysm   _____

    Hypertensive cardiovascular disease, essential   _____

    Procedure: Resection of abdominal aortic aneurysm
    w/graft replacement   _____

11. Rectal polyp   _____

    Procedure: Colonoscopy with polypectomy   _____

12. Pilonidal fistula with abscess   _____

    Procedure: Excision of pilondial cyst   _____

13. Menometrorrhagia, endometrial polyp, corpus luteum
    cysts of both ovaries

    _____ _____ _____

    Procedure: Total abdominal hysterectomy; bilateral
    salpingo-oophorectomy

    _____ _____

14. Squamous cell carcinoma in situ, floor of mouth

    _____

    Procedure: Resection of lesion, floor of mouth

    _____

15. Iron deficiency anemia, 6-month pregnant female

    _____

    Procedure: Transfusion of two units packed cells

    _____

REVIEW QUESTIONS

1. Match the following abbreviations with their meaning.

   _____ DRG
   _____ CMS 1500
   _____ UB-92
   _____ UHDDS
   _____ CMI
   _____ IPPS

   a. Data set for hospital inpatient coding
   b. Medicare reimbursement for inpatient coding
   c. Diagnosis classification for reimbursement
   d. Billing form for physician/outpatient services
   e. Billing form for hospital claims
   f. Inpatient information data for third-party payers

2. Which one of the following is a symptom?
   a. Abdominal pain
   b. Laceration of finger
   c. Rash on forehead
   d. Swelling of eye

3. What is the term for chronic conditions the patient had before a specific admission?
   a. Comorbidity
   b. Complication
   c. Diagnosis related group
   d. Major diagnostic category

4. What is the main goal or purpose of the Medicare Program Integrity provision established by CMS?
   a. To coordinate the assignment of the National Provider Identification number
   b. To pay claims correctly and investigate claims in violation of CMS regulations
   c. To provide guidelines for diagnosis related groups
   d. To standardize the CMS-1500 and UB-92 forms

5. What term is used to identify a patient who is discharged following hospital stay with transfer to a nursing facility?
   a. Disposition
   b. Length of stay
   c. Medical necessity
   d. Unconfirmed condition

Appendix A

Certification Practice

The following is a mock examination providing practice for certification for professional medical coders, the Certified Professional Coder (CPC), as offered by the American Academy of Professional Coders (AAPC). A practice examination allows the student to recognize individual strengths and weaknesses to prepare for the examination.

ICD-9-CM, CPT, and HCPCS coding books are necessary for this exam. The CPC exam is a 5-hour exam in three sections in the following format:

Section 1: Medical Concepts (43 questions)
    Medical Terminology (13)
    Anatomy (9)
    ICD-9-CM (11)
    HCPCS (5)
    Coding Concepts (5)

Section 2: Surgery and Modifiers (60 questions)
    10000 (9)
    20000 (10)
    30000 (10)
    40000 (10)
    50000 (11)
    60000 (10)

Section 3: Other areas of CPT (47 questions)
    Evaluation and Management (12)
    Anesthesia (6)
    Radiology (9)
    Laboratory and Pathology (10)
    Medicine (10)

Certification Practice

Choose the best answer for each of the following scenarios.

1. What are the three key components for E/M services?
    a. Decision making, counseling, coordination of care
    b. History, physical exam, decision making
    c. Physical exam, decision making, time
    d. Physical exam, counseling, time

2. What condition do the acronyms IDDM and NIDDM relate to?
   a. Arthritis
   b. Cardiovascular disease
   c. Diabetes
   d. Pregnancy

3. How many codes are required to code internal and external hemorrhoids that are bleeding?
   a. 1
   b. 2
   c. 3
   d. 4

4. In coding the diagnosis carcinoma of the liver metastatic to the pancreas, what does metastatic mean?
   a. The liver is a secondary site.
   b. The pancreas is the primary site.
   c. The pancreas is a secondary site.
   d. It is unspecified.

5. What does the term epistaxis mean?
   a. Headache
   b. Heartburn
   c. Hives
   d. Nosebleed

6. A patient is seen by the PCP for a skin lesion of the right cheek, which is documented as probable melanoma. The patient is referred to a dermatologist for evaluation of the lesion. What is the ICD-9-CM code for the PCP to submit to the insurance carrier?
   a. 172.3
   b. 172.8
   c. 528.9
   d. 709.9

7. What is an example of an intermediate joint?
   a. Elbow
   b. Hip
   c. Knee
   d. Shoulder

8. A patient is diagnosed with carcinoma in situ of the breast. There is a family history of lung cancer. What are the correct codes?
   a. 174.9, V10.3
   b. 174.9, V16.1
   c. 233.0, V16.1
   d. 233.0, V10.3

9. What is meant by a disease or condition that is congenital?
   a. It is contagious.
   b. It develops soon after birth.
   c. It is present or existing at birth.
   d. It is a secondary disease or condition.

10. Where are the codes located for services provided by an urgent or immediate care center?
    a. Appendix A of CPT
    b. Emergency room services of CPT
    c. Office or other outpatient services of CPT
    d. Volume 3 of ICD-9-CM

11. What is the medical service for follow-up of a patient initially in the office for a consultation?
    a. Established patient office visit
    b. Follow-up consultation
    c. Initial consultation
    d. Referral consultation

12. Which one of the following is *not* an example of an E code?
    a. Drowning in a bathtub
    b. Falling off a horse
    c. Family history of alcoholism
    d. Overdose of Sudafed

13. What is the code for an electroencephalogram, monitored for 55 minutes?
    a. 95812
    b. 95813
    c. 95816
    d. 95819

14. A 6-month-old infant has an initial inguinal herniorrhaphy. What is the code for the anesthesia services for this procedure?
    a. 00830
    b. 00832
    c. 00834, 99100
    d. 00836, 99100

15. What section of CPT contains the codes for therapeutic injection services?
    a. Anesthesia
    b. Evaluation and Management
    c. Medicine
    d. Radiology/Laboratory/Pathology

16. What anatomical section is affected by COPD?
    a. Extremities
    b. Intestines
    c. Lungs
    d. Stomach

17. What are the codes for a patient admitted for an initial acute MI of inferoposterior wall, CHF, and hypertension?
    a. 410.21, 428.0, 401.9
    b. 410.31, 428.0, 401.9
    c. 410.40, 428.0, 401.9
    d. 410.80, 428.0, 401.9

18. What codes are found in the Special Services and Reports of the Medicine Section of CPT?
    a. Immunizations and injections
    b. Laboratory/radiology/laboratory
    c. Preventive medicine
    d. Supplies, handling of specimens, medical testimony, unusual services

19. A patient is admitted at 11:00 a.m. by the surgeon for observation following a septoplasty and is discharged at 3:00 p.m. He is seen in follow-up one week later by the surgeon. What are the appropriate codes to submit for the surgeon's services?
    a. 30520
    b. 30520, 99212
    c. 30520, 99234, 99238
    d. 30520, 99234, 99238, 99212

20. Which one of the following is an example of a symptom?
    a. Back pain
    b. Fracture of left tibia
    c. Laceration of right index finger
    d. Rash on forehead

21. What code is assigned for a work-related examination/evaluation by a physician other than the treating physician for the patient?
    a. 99056
    b. 99273
    c. 99455
    d. 99456

22. A patient has a urine pregnancy test performed by the lab using a visual color comparison test. This is coded
    a. 81025
    b. 81025, 36415
    c. 81025, 99000
    d. 84702

23. Which one of the following is an x-ray of the urinary tract?
    a. CABG
    b. IPPB
    c. KUB
    d. TURP

24. A physician sends a patient to the lab with an order for an electrolyte panel and a glucose. What are the correct codes for the lab to bill?
    a. 80048
    b. 80051, 82947
    c. 80053
    d. 82374, 82435, 82947, 84132, 84295

25. A 26-year-old female who is 4 months pregnant has Type II diabetes. This is her first pregnancy. There are no complications and the pregnancy is normal.
    a. 250.00, V22.0
    b. 250.02, V22.0

   c. 648.80, V22.0

   d. 250.00, V22.2

26. A patient is treated in the Urgent Care Center for a laceration of the chin requiring simple repair of a 3 cm. wound. The visit today is a problem-focused history and exam of straightforward medical decision making. The patient is visiting relatives locally and has not been treated in this facility prior to this incident. He is told to see his physician when he returns home. What are the correct codes to bill for this encounter?

   a. 99201, 12002

   b. 99201, 12013

   c. 99281, 12013

   d. 99288, 12013

27. What is the medical term for difficulty with swallowing?

   a. Dyspepsia

   b. Dysphagia

   c. Dysphasia

   d. Dyspnea

28. Which one of the following is related to the term ESRD?

   a. Raynaud's disease

   b. Renal disease

   c. Respiratory distress

   d. Retinal disorder

29. A patient's chart is noted of a history of penicillin allergy.

   a. V14.0

   b. V14.1

   c. V14.3

   d. 995.2

30. A physician orders a total serum cholesterol, lipoprotein, high density cholesterol, and triglycerides.

   a. 80061

   b. 82465, 83715, 84478

   c. 82465, 83716, 84478

   d. 82465, 83718, 84478

31. What is the medical term for incision of the vulva, usually done during labor to avoid laceration of the perineum during delivery?

   a. Colporrhaphy

   b. Episiotomy

   c. Orchiotomy

   d. Orchiopexy

32. When a consultation is required for confirmation by a third-party payer, such as Medicare, what is the modifier to use to indicate this with the appropriate CPT code?

   a. -21

   b. -22

   c. -26

   d. -32

33. Which of the following are *not* bones in the hand?
    a. Carpals
    b. Metacarpals
    c. Phalanges
    d. Tarsals

34. An established patient is seen in the office for a detailed history and exam for uncontrolled IDDM. His glucose levels checked at home have been running between 350–475. The patient also has cataracts related to his diabetic condition. What are the codes for this encounter?
    a. 99203, 250.53, 366.41
    b. 99214, 250.53, 366.41
    c. 99214, 250.00, 366.41
    d. 99214, 366.41, 250.53

35. Which one of the following is an eponym?
    a. Acquired immune deficiency syndrome
    b. Arteriosclerotic cardiovascular disease
    c. Huntington's chorea
    d. Poliomyelitis

36. A patient becomes agitated in the office and is given Valium 10 mg. IM. What is the correct code for the medication?
    a. J2860
    b. J3360
    c. J3360 x 2
    d. J3490 x 2

37. A patient returns to the office for recheck of recently diagnosed pernicious anemia. The exam today is problem focused, and she is given an injection of B12 500 mg. IM. What are the correct codes?
    a. 99202, 90772, J3420, 281.0
    b. 99212, 90772, J3420, 281.0
    c. 99212, 90772, J3420, 281.1
    d. 99212, 90772, J3420, 285.1

38. A new patient is seen for multiple skin tags of the back of the neck and upper back/shoulder area. The office visit was expanded problem focused with straightforward decision making. Ten skin tags were removed by scissoring with electrocauterization of the sites. What are the correct codes?
    a. 99202, 11200
    b. 99202-25, 11200
    c. 99202-25, 11200, 11201
    d. 99213, 11200

39. What is the medical term for hives?
    a. Pediculosis
    b. Tinea corporis
    c. Urticaria
    d. Verrucae

40. What does alopecia mean?
    a. Acne
    b. Hair loss

c. Ringworm

d. Shingles

41. A 19-year-old male is diagnosed with noise-induced hearing loss from exposure to continuous loud music from MP3. What code indicates this?

    a. 388.12

    b. 389.14

    c. 389.8

    d. 389.9

42. What is meant by the term "etiology undetermined" when a physician describes signs or symptoms?

    a. Cause is unknown

    b. Caused by disease

    c. Caused by treatment

    d. No medical reason

43. A patient is followed in the nursing home for aphasia and hemiplegia following a CVA 2 years ago. How is this coded?

    a. 434.91, 438.11, 438.20

    b. 438.11, 438.20

    c. 438.82, 438.20

    d. 438.9

44. A 5-year-old child is seen in the office for routine well-child check. The family is new to this practice. She is also given MMR and oral polio vaccinations. The exam and history today are EPF with straightforward medical decision making.

    a. 99202, 90707, 90712, 90471, 90474

    b. 99383, 90707, 90712, 90471, 90474

    c. 99383, 90707, 90710, 90465, 90467

    d. 99393, 90707, 90712, 90471, 90474

45. A myringotomy is performed on a 3-year-old child with acute otitis media. How is this coded?

    a. 382.9, 69420

    b. 382.9, 69421

    c. 382.9, 69620

    d. 382.00, 69420

46. A 17-year-old female is admitted for anorexia nervosa with continuous habitual use of laxatives. How is this coded?

    a. 307.1, 305.91

    b. 307.1, 305.9

    c. 783.0, 305.91

    d. 995.84

47. A patient is seen in the GYN clinic for insertion of an IUD for birth control measures. She was seen one month ago for gynecological exam and Pap smear and counseling for the procedure. How is this coded?

    a. 58300, V25.02

    b. 58300, V25.1

    c. 58300, V25.41

    d. 58300, V25.42

48. A new patient is seen in the office for a detailed history and exam with direct admission from the office to the hospital for herpes ophthalmicus zoster. The admission is documented as a comprehensive history and exam with medical decision making of moderate complexity. He is followed in the hospital for two days, EPF. The following day, the physician spends 45 minutes in discharge services for the patient. How is this coded?

    a. 99203, 99222, 99232 x 2, 99239

    b. 99203, 99229, 99217

    c. 99222, 99232 x 2, 99239

    d. 99203, 99235, 99239

49. What are Braxton-Hicks contractions?

    a. Abdominal cramps

    b. Bladder spasms

    c. False labor pains

    d. Miscarriage

50. A patient has a colonoscopy because of a family history of colon cancer. During the procedure, two small polyps are removed by snare technique. How is this coded?

    a. 45315, V16.0

    b. 45338, V16.0, 211.3

    c. 45378, V16.0

    d. 45385, V16.0, 211.3

PLEASE
DO NOT
STAPLE
IN THIS
AREA

HEALTH INSURANCE CLAIM FORM

| PICA | | | | | | | | PICA | |

1. MEDICARE   MEDICAID   CHAMPUS   CHAMPVA   GROUP HEALTH PLAN   FECA BLK LUNG   OTHER   1a. INSURED'S I.D. NUMBER   (FOR PROGRAM IN ITEM 1)

(Medicare #)   (Medicaid #)   (Sponsor's SSN)   (VA File #)   (SSN or ID)   (SSN)   (ID)

2. PATIENT'S NAME (Last Name, First Name, Middle Initial)

3. PATIENT'S BIRTH DATE   MM   DD   YY   SEX   M   F

4. INSURED'S NAME (Last Name, First Name, Middle Initial)

5. PATIENT'S ADDRESS (No., Street)

6. PATIENT RELATIONSHIP TO INSURED   Self   Spouse   Child   Other

7. INSURED'S ADDRESS (No., Street)

CITY   STATE

8. PATIENT STATUS   Single   Married   Other

CITY   STATE

ZIP CODE   TELEPHONE (Include Area Code)   (   )

Employed   Full-Time Student   Part-Time Student

ZIP CODE   TELEPHONE (INCLUDE AREA CODE)   (   )

9. OTHER INSURED'S NAME (Last Name, First Name, Middle Initial)

10. IS PATIENT'S CONDITION RELATED TO:

11. INSURED'S POLICY GROUP OR FECA NUMBER

a. OTHER INSURED'S POLICY OR GROUP NUMBER

a. EMPLOYMENT? (CURRENT OR PREVIOUS)   YES   NO

a. INSURED'S DATE OF BIRTH   MM   DD   YY   SEX   M   F

b. OTHER INSURED'S DATE OF BIRTH   MM   DD   YY   SEX   M   F

b. AUTO ACCIDENT?   PLACE (State)   YES   NO

b. EMPLOYER'S NAME OR SCHOOL NAME

c. EMPLOYER'S NAME OR SCHOOL NAME

c. OTHER ACCIDENT?   YES   NO

c. INSURANCE PLAN NAME OR PROGRAM NAME

d. INSURANCE PLAN NAME OR PROGRAM NAME

10d. RESERVED FOR LOCAL USE

d. IS THERE ANOTHER HEALTH BENEFIT PLAN?   YES   NO   **If yes**, return to and complete item 9 a-d.

READ BACK OF FORM BEFORE COMPLETING & SIGNING THIS FORM.

12. PATIENT'S OR AUTHORIZED PERSON'S SIGNATURE I authorize the release of any medical or other information necessary to process this claim. I also request payment of government benefits either to myself or to the party who accepts assignment below.

SIGNED _____   DATE _____

13. INSURED'S OR AUTHORIZED PERSON'S SIGNATURE I authorize payment of medical benefits to the undersigned physician or supplier for services described below.

SIGNED _____

14. DATE OF CURRENT: MM   DD   YY   ◀ ILLNESS (First symptom) OR INJURY (Accident) OR PREGNANCY(LMP)

15. IF PATIENT HAS HAD SAME OR SIMILAR ILLNESS. GIVE FIRST DATE   MM   DD   YY

16. DATES PATIENT UNABLE TO WORK IN CURRENT OCCUPATION   MM   DD   YY   FROM   TO   MM   DD   YY

17. NAME OF REFERRING PHYSICIAN OR OTHER SOURCE

17a. I.D. NUMBER OF REFERRING PHYSICIAN

18. HOSPITALIZATION DATES RELATED TO CURRENT SERVICES   MM   DD   YY   FROM   TO   MM   DD   YY

19. RESERVED FOR LOCAL USE

20. OUTSIDE LAB?   YES   NO $ CHARGES

21. DIAGNOSIS OR NATURE OF ILLNESS OR INJURY. (RELATE ITEMS 1,2,3 OR 4 TO ITEM 24E BY LINE)

1. └___.___   3. └___.___

2. └___.___   4. └___.___

22. MEDICAID RESUBMISSION CODE   ORIGINAL REF. NO.

23. PRIOR AUTHORIZATION NUMBER

24. A DATE(S) OF SERVICE						B Place of Service	C Type of Service	D PROCEDURES, SERVICES, OR SUPPLIES (Explain Unusual Circumstances) CPT/HCPCS | MODIFIER	E DIAGNOSIS CODE	F $ CHARGES	G DAYS OR UNITS	H EPSDT Family Plan	I EMG	J COB	K RESERVED FOR LOCAL USE
From MM	DD	YY	To MM	DD	YY										
1															
2															
3															
4															
5															
6															

25. FEDERAL TAX I.D. NUMBER   SSN   EIN

26. PATIENT'S ACCOUNT NO.

27. ACCEPT ASSIGNMENT? (For govt. claims, see back)   YES   NO

28. TOTAL CHARGE $

29. AMOUNT PAID $

30. BALANCE DUE $

31. SIGNATURE OF PHYSICIAN OR SUPPLIER INCLUDING DEGREES OR CREDENTIALS (I certify that the statements on the reverse apply to this bill and are made a part thereof.)

SIGNED _____   DATE _____

32. NAME AND ADDRESS OF FACILITY WHERE SERVICES WERE RENDERED (If other than home or office)

33. PHYSICIAN'S, SUPPLIER'S BILLING NAME, ADDRESS, ZIP CODE & PHONE #

PIN#   GRP#

PLEASE
DO NOT
STAPLE
IN THIS
AREA

| | PICA | | | | | **HEALTH INSURANCE CLAIM FORM** | | PICA | | |

HEALTH INSURANCE CLAIM FORM

1. MEDICARE	MEDICAID	CHAMPUS	CHAMPVA	GROUP HEALTH PLAN (SSN or ID)	FECA BLK LUNG (SSN)	OTHER	1a. INSURED'S I.D. NUMBER (FOR PROGRAM IN ITEM 1)
(Medicare #)	(Medicaid #)	(Sponsor's SSN)	(VA File #)			(ID)	

2. PATIENT'S NAME (Last Name, First Name, Middle Initial)

3. PATIENT'S BIRTH DATE MM DD YY   SEX   M ☐ F ☐

4. INSURED'S NAME (Last Name, First Name, Middle Initial)

5. PATIENT'S ADDRESS (No., Street)

6. PATIENT RELATIONSHIP TO INSURED Self ☐ Spouse ☐ Child ☐ Other ☐

7. INSURED'S ADDRESS (No., Street)

CITY   STATE

8. PATIENT STATUS Single ☐ Married ☐ Other ☐

CITY   STATE

ZIP CODE   TELEPHONE (Include Area Code) (   )

Employed ☐ Full-Time Student ☐ Part-Time Student ☐

ZIP CODE   TELEPHONE (INCLUDE AREA CODE) (   )

9. OTHER INSURED'S NAME (Last Name, First Name, Middle Initial)

10. IS PATIENT'S CONDITION RELATED TO:

11. INSURED'S POLICY GROUP OR FECA NUMBER

a. OTHER INSURED'S POLICY OR GROUP NUMBER

a. EMPLOYMENT? (CURRENT OR PREVIOUS) ☐ YES ☐ NO

a. INSURED'S DATE OF BIRTH MM DD YY   SEX   M ☐ F ☐

b. OTHER INSURED'S DATE OF BIRTH MM DD YY   SEX M ☐ F ☐

b. AUTO ACCIDENT?   PLACE (State) ☐ YES ☐ NO

b. EMPLOYER'S NAME OR SCHOOL NAME

c. EMPLOYER'S NAME OR SCHOOL NAME

c. OTHER ACCIDENT? ☐ YES ☐ NO

c. INSURANCE PLAN NAME OR PROGRAM NAME

d. INSURANCE PLAN NAME OR PROGRAM NAME

10d. RESERVED FOR LOCAL USE

d. IS THERE ANOTHER HEALTH BENEFIT PLAN? ☐ YES ☐ NO *If yes,* return to and complete item 9 a-d.

READ BACK OF FORM BEFORE COMPLETING & SIGNING THIS FORM.

12. PATIENT'S OR AUTHORIZED PERSON'S SIGNATURE I authorize the release of any medical or other information necessary to process this claim. I also request payment of government benefits either to myself or to the party who accepts assignment below.

SIGNED _____ DATE _____

13. INSURED'S OR AUTHORIZED PERSON'S SIGNATURE I authorize payment of medical benefits to the undersigned physician or supplier for services described below.

SIGNED _____

14. DATE OF CURRENT: MM DD YY ◀ ILLNESS (First symptom) OR INJURY (Accident) OR PREGNANCY(LMP)

15. IF PATIENT HAS HAD SAME OR SIMILAR ILLNESS. GIVE FIRST DATE MM DD YY

16. DATES PATIENT UNABLE TO WORK IN CURRENT OCCUPATION FROM MM DD YY TO MM DD YY

17. NAME OF REFERRING PHYSICIAN OR OTHER SOURCE

17a. I.D. NUMBER OF REFERRING PHYSICIAN

18. HOSPITALIZATION DATES RELATED TO CURRENT SERVICES FROM MM DD YY TO MM DD YY

19. RESERVED FOR LOCAL USE

20. OUTSIDE LAB? ☐ YES ☐ NO $ CHARGES

21. DIAGNOSIS OR NATURE OF ILLNESS OR INJURY. (RELATE ITEMS 1,2,3 OR 4 TO ITEM 24E BY LINE)

1. L___.___   3. L___.___

2. L___.___   4. L___.___

22. MEDICAID RESUBMISSION CODE   ORIGINAL REF. NO.

23. PRIOR AUTHORIZATION NUMBER

24. A DATE(S) OF SERVICE						B Place of Service	C Type of Service	D PROCEDURES, SERVICES, OR SUPPLIES (Explain Unusual Circumstances) CPT/HCPCS MODIFIER	E DIAGNOSIS CODE	F $ CHARGES	G DAYS OR UNITS	H EPSDT Family Plan	I EMG	J COB	K RESERVED FOR LOCAL USE
From MM	DD	YY	To MM	DD	YY										
1															
2															
3															
4															
5															
6															

25. FEDERAL TAX I.D. NUMBER SSN ☐ EIN ☐

26. PATIENT'S ACCOUNT NO.

27. ACCEPT ASSIGNMENT? (For govt. claims, see back) ☐ YES ☐ NO

28. TOTAL CHARGE $

29. AMOUNT PAID $

30. BALANCE DUE $

31. SIGNATURE OF PHYSICIAN OR SUPPLIER INCLUDING DEGREES OR CREDENTIALS (I certify that the statements on the reverse apply to this bill and are made a part thereof.)

SIGNED _____ DATE _____

32. NAME AND ADDRESS OF FACILITY WHERE SERVICES WERE RENDERED (If other than home or office)

33. PHYSICIAN'S, SUPPLIER'S BILLING NAME, ADDRESS, ZIP CODE & PHONE #

PIN#   GRP#

(APPROVED BY AMA COUNCIL ON MEDICAL SERVICE 8/88) **PLEASE PRINT OR TYPE** APPROVED OMB-0938-0008 FORM CMS-1500 (12/90), FORM RRB-1500
APPROVED OMB-1215-0055 FORM OWCP-1500, APPROVED OMB-0720-0001 (CHAMPUS)

PLEASE
DO NOT
STAPLE
IN THIS
AREA

CARRIER →

HEALTH INSURANCE CLAIM FORM

| | | PICA | | | | | | | | PICA | | |

1. MEDICARE (Medicare #)   **MEDICAID** (Medicaid #)   **CHAMPUS** (Sponsor's SSN)   **CHAMPVA** (VA File #)   **GROUP HEALTH PLAN** (SSN or ID)   **FECA BLK LUNG** (SSN)   **OTHER** (ID)

1a. INSURED'S I.D. NUMBER   (FOR PROGRAM IN ITEM 1)

2. PATIENT'S NAME (Last Name, First Name, Middle Initial)

3. PATIENT'S BIRTH DATE   MM   DD   YY   **SEX**   M ☐   F ☐

4. INSURED'S NAME (Last Name, First Name, Middle Initial)

5. PATIENT'S ADDRESS (No., Street)

6. PATIENT RELATIONSHIP TO INSURED   Self ☐   Spouse ☐   Child ☐   Other ☐

7. INSURED'S ADDRESS (No., Street)

CITY   STATE

8. PATIENT STATUS   Single ☐   Married ☐   Other ☐   Employed ☐   Full-Time Student ☐   Part-Time Student ☐

CITY   STATE

ZIP CODE   TELEPHONE (Include Area Code)   ( )

ZIP CODE   TELEPHONE (INCLUDE AREA CODE)   ( )

9. OTHER INSURED'S NAME (Last Name, First Name, Middle Initial)

10. IS PATIENT'S CONDITION RELATED TO:

11. INSURED'S POLICY GROUP OR FECA NUMBER

a. OTHER INSURED'S POLICY OR GROUP NUMBER

a. EMPLOYMENT? (CURRENT OR PREVIOUS)   YES ☐   NO ☐

a. INSURED'S DATE OF BIRTH   MM   DD   YY   **SEX**   M ☐   F ☐

b. OTHER INSURED'S DATE OF BIRTH   MM   DD   YY   **SEX**   M ☐   F ☐

b. AUTO ACCIDENT?   PLACE (State)   YES ☐   NO ☐

b. EMPLOYER'S NAME OR SCHOOL NAME

c. EMPLOYER'S NAME OR SCHOOL NAME

c. OTHER ACCIDENT?   YES ☐   NO ☐

c. INSURANCE PLAN NAME OR PROGRAM NAME

d. INSURANCE PLAN NAME OR PROGRAM NAME

10d. RESERVED FOR LOCAL USE

d. IS THERE ANOTHER HEALTH BENEFIT PLAN?   YES ☐   NO ☐   *If yes*, return to and complete item 9 a-d.

READ BACK OF FORM BEFORE COMPLETING & SIGNING THIS FORM.

12. PATIENT'S OR AUTHORIZED PERSON'S SIGNATURE I authorize the release of any medical or other information necessary to process this claim. I also request payment of government benefits either to myself or to the party who accepts assignment below.

SIGNED _____ DATE _____

13. INSURED'S OR AUTHORIZED PERSON'S SIGNATURE I authorize payment of medical benefits to the undersigned physician or supplier for services described below.

SIGNED _____

14. DATE OF CURRENT: ◄ ILLNESS (First symptom) OR INJURY (Accident) OR PREGNANCY(LMP)   MM   DD   YY

15. IF PATIENT HAS HAD SAME OR SIMILAR ILLNESS. GIVE FIRST DATE   MM   DD   YY

16. DATES PATIENT UNABLE TO WORK IN CURRENT OCCUPATION   FROM   MM   DD   YY   TO   MM   DD   YY

17. NAME OF REFERRING PHYSICIAN OR OTHER SOURCE

17a. I.D. NUMBER OF REFERRING PHYSICIAN

18. HOSPITALIZATION DATES RELATED TO CURRENT SERVICES   FROM   MM   DD   YY   TO   MM   DD   YY

19. RESERVED FOR LOCAL USE

20. OUTSIDE LAB?   YES ☐   NO ☐ $ CHARGES

21. DIAGNOSIS OR NATURE OF ILLNESS OR INJURY. (RELATE ITEMS 1,2,3 OR 4 TO ITEM 24E BY LINE)

1. L___.___
2. L___.___
3. L___.___
4. L___.___

22. MEDICAID RESUBMISSION CODE   ORIGINAL REF. NO.

23. PRIOR AUTHORIZATION NUMBER

24.	A DATE(S) OF SERVICE					B Place of Service	C Type of Service	D PROCEDURES, SERVICES, OR SUPPLIES (Explain Unusual Circumstances) CPT/HCPCS	MODIFIER	E DIAGNOSIS CODE	F $ CHARGES	G DAYS OR UNITS	H EPSDT Family Plan	I EMG	J COB	K RESERVED FOR LOCAL USE
	From MM	DD	YY	To MM	DD	YY											
1																	
2																	
3																	
4																	
5																	
6																	

25. FEDERAL TAX I.D. NUMBER   SSN ☐ EIN ☐

26. PATIENT'S ACCOUNT NO.

27. ACCEPT ASSIGNMENT? (For govt. claims, see back)   YES ☐   NO ☐

28. TOTAL CHARGE $

29. AMOUNT PAID $

30. BALANCE DUE $

31. SIGNATURE OF PHYSICIAN OR SUPPLIER INCLUDING DEGREES OR CREDENTIALS (I certify that the statements on the reverse apply to this bill and are made a part thereof.)

SIGNED _____ DATE _____

32. NAME AND ADDRESS OF FACILITY WHERE SERVICES WERE RENDERED (If other than home or office)

33. PHYSICIAN'S, SUPPLIER'S BILLING NAME, ADDRESS, ZIP CODE & PHONE #

PIN# _____   GRP# _____

(APPROVED BY AMA COUNCIL ON MEDICAL SERVICE 8/88)   **PLEASE PRINT OR TYPE**

APPROVED OMB-0938-0008 FORM CMS-1500 (12/90), FORM RRB-1500
APPROVED OMB-1215-0055 FORM OWCP-1500, APPROVED OMB-0720-0001 (CHAMPUS)

PATIENT AND INSURED INFORMATION →

PHYSICIAN OR SUPPLIER INFORMATION →

PLEASE
DO NOT
STAPLE
IN THIS
AREA

CARRIER →

[ ][ ] PICA

HEALTH INSURANCE CLAIM FORM

PICA [ ][ ]

1. MEDICARE [ ] (Medicare #) MEDICAID [ ] (Medicaid #) CHAMPUS [ ] (Sponsor's SSN) CHAMPVA [ ] (VA File #) GROUP HEALTH PLAN [ ] (SSN or ID) FECA BLK LUNG [ ] (SSN) OTHER [ ] (ID)

1a. INSURED'S I.D. NUMBER   (FOR PROGRAM IN ITEM 1)

2. PATIENT'S NAME (Last Name, First Name, Middle Initial)

3. PATIENT'S BIRTH DATE MM | DD | YY   SEX   M [ ] F [ ]

4. INSURED'S NAME (Last Name, First Name, Middle Initial)

5. PATIENT'S ADDRESS (No., Street)

6. PATIENT RELATIONSHIP TO INSURED   Self [ ] Spouse [ ] Child [ ] Other [ ]

7. INSURED'S ADDRESS (No., Street)

CITY   STATE

8. PATIENT STATUS   Single [ ] Married [ ] Other [ ]

Employed [ ] Full-Time Student [ ] Part-Time Student [ ]

CITY   STATE

ZIP CODE   TELEPHONE (Include Area Code) (   )

ZIP CODE   TELEPHONE (INCLUDE AREA CODE) (   )

9. OTHER INSURED'S NAME (Last Name, First Name, Middle Initial)

10. IS PATIENT'S CONDITION RELATED TO:

11. INSURED'S POLICY GROUP OR FECA NUMBER

a. OTHER INSURED'S POLICY OR GROUP NUMBER

a. EMPLOYMENT? (CURRENT OR PREVIOUS) YES [ ] NO [ ]

a. INSURED'S DATE OF BIRTH MM | DD | YY   SEX M [ ] F [ ]

b. OTHER INSURED'S DATE OF BIRTH MM | DD | YY   SEX M [ ] F [ ]

b. AUTO ACCIDENT?   PLACE (State) YES [ ] NO [ ]

b. EMPLOYER'S NAME OR SCHOOL NAME

c. EMPLOYER'S NAME OR SCHOOL NAME

c. OTHER ACCIDENT? YES [ ] NO [ ]

c. INSURANCE PLAN NAME OR PROGRAM NAME

d. INSURANCE PLAN NAME OR PROGRAM NAME

10d. RESERVED FOR LOCAL USE

d. IS THERE ANOTHER HEALTH BENEFIT PLAN? YES [ ] NO [ ] If yes, return to and complete item 9 a-d.

READ BACK OF FORM BEFORE COMPLETING & SIGNING THIS FORM.
12. PATIENT'S OR AUTHORIZED PERSON'S SIGNATURE I authorize the release of any medical or other information necessary to process this claim. I also request payment of government benefits either to myself or to the party who accepts assignment below.

SIGNED _____ DATE _____

13. INSURED'S OR AUTHORIZED PERSON'S SIGNATURE I authorize payment of medical benefits to the undersigned physician or supplier for services described below.

SIGNED _____

14. DATE OF CURRENT: MM | DD | YY ILLNESS (First symptom) OR INJURY (Accident) OR PREGNANCY(LMP)

15. IF PATIENT HAS HAD SAME OR SIMILAR ILLNESS. GIVE FIRST DATE MM | DD | YY

16. DATES PATIENT UNABLE TO WORK IN CURRENT OCCUPATION FROM MM | DD | YY TO MM | DD | YY

17. NAME OF REFERRING PHYSICIAN OR OTHER SOURCE

17a. I.D. NUMBER OF REFERRING PHYSICIAN

18. HOSPITALIZATION DATES RELATED TO CURRENT SERVICES FROM MM | DD | YY TO MM | DD | YY

19. RESERVED FOR LOCAL USE

20. OUTSIDE LAB? YES [ ] NO [ ] $ CHARGES

21. DIAGNOSIS OR NATURE OF ILLNESS OR INJURY. (RELATE ITEMS 1,2,3 OR 4 TO ITEM 24E BY LINE)
1. |___.___ 3. |___.___
2. |___.___ 4. |___.___

22. MEDICAID RESUBMISSION CODE   ORIGINAL REF. NO.

23. PRIOR AUTHORIZATION NUMBER

24. A DATE(S) OF SERVICE From MM DD YY To MM DD YY	B Place of Service	C Type of Service	D PROCEDURES, SERVICES, OR SUPPLIES (Explain Unusual Circumstances) CPT/HCPCS	MODIFIER	E DIAGNOSIS CODE	F $ CHARGES	G DAYS OR UNITS	H EPSDT Family Plan	I EMG	J COB	K RESERVED FOR LOCAL USE
1											
2											
3											
4											
5											
6											

25. FEDERAL TAX I.D. NUMBER SSN [ ] EIN [ ]

26. PATIENT'S ACCOUNT NO.

27. ACCEPT ASSIGNMENT? (For govt. claims, see back) YES [ ] NO [ ]

28. TOTAL CHARGE $

29. AMOUNT PAID $

30. BALANCE DUE $

31. SIGNATURE OF PHYSICIAN OR SUPPLIER INCLUDING DEGREES OR CREDENTIALS (I certify that the statements on the reverse apply to this bill and are made a part thereof.)

SIGNED _____ DATE _____

32. NAME AND ADDRESS OF FACILITY WHERE SERVICES WERE RENDERED (If other than home or office)

33. PHYSICIAN'S, SUPPLIER'S BILLING NAME, ADDRESS, ZIP CODE & PHONE #

PIN# _____ GRP# _____

(APPROVED BY AMA COUNCIL ON MEDICAL SERVICE 8/88) **PLEASE PRINT OR TYPE** APPROVED OMB-0938-0008 FORM CMS-1500 (12/90), FORM RRB-1500 APPROVED OMB-1215-0055 FORM OWCP-1500, APPROVED OMB-0720-0001 (CHAMPUS)

PATIENT AND INSURED INFORMATION

PHYSICIAN OR SUPPLIER INFORMATION

PLEASE
DO NOT
STAPLE
IN THIS
AREA

HEALTH INSURANCE CLAIM FORM

| | PICA | | | | | | | | | | PICA | | |

1. MEDICARE	MEDICAID	CHAMPUS	CHAMPVA	GROUP HEALTH PLAN	FECA BLK LUNG	OTHER	1a. INSURED'S I.D. NUMBER	(FOR PROGRAM IN ITEM 1)
(Medicare #)	(Medicaid #)	(Sponsor's SSN)	(VA File #)	(SSN or ID)	(SSN)	(ID)		

2. PATIENT'S NAME (Last Name, First Name, Middle Initial)

3. PATIENT'S BIRTH DATE   MM   DD   YY   SEX   M   F

4. INSURED'S NAME (Last Name, First Name, Middle Initial)

5. PATIENT'S ADDRESS (No., Street)

6. PATIENT RELATIONSHIP TO INSURED   Self   Spouse   Child   Other

7. INSURED'S ADDRESS (No., Street)

CITY   STATE

8. PATIENT STATUS   Single   Married   Other

CITY   STATE

ZIP CODE   TELEPHONE (Include Area Code)   (   )

Employed   Full-Time Student   Part-Time Student

ZIP CODE   TELEPHONE (INCLUDE AREA CODE)   (   )

9. OTHER INSURED'S NAME (Last Name, First Name, Middle Initial)

10. IS PATIENT'S CONDITION RELATED TO:

11. INSURED'S POLICY GROUP OR FECA NUMBER

a. OTHER INSURED'S POLICY OR GROUP NUMBER

a. EMPLOYMENT? (CURRENT OR PREVIOUS)   YES   NO

a. INSURED'S DATE OF BIRTH   MM   DD   YY   SEX   M   F

b. OTHER INSURED'S DATE OF BIRTH   MM   DD   YY   SEX   M   F

b. AUTO ACCIDENT?   PLACE (State)   YES   NO

b. EMPLOYER'S NAME OR SCHOOL NAME

c. EMPLOYER'S NAME OR SCHOOL NAME

c. OTHER ACCIDENT?   YES   NO

c. INSURANCE PLAN NAME OR PROGRAM NAME

d. INSURANCE PLAN NAME OR PROGRAM NAME

10d. RESERVED FOR LOCAL USE

d. IS THERE ANOTHER HEALTH BENEFIT PLAN?   YES   NO   If yes, return to and complete item 9 a-d.

READ BACK OF FORM BEFORE COMPLETING & SIGNING THIS FORM.

12. PATIENT'S OR AUTHORIZED PERSON'S SIGNATURE I authorize the release of any medical or other information necessary to process this claim. I also request payment of government benefits either to myself or to the party who accepts assignment below.

SIGNED _____   DATE _____

13. INSURED'S OR AUTHORIZED PERSON'S SIGNATURE I authorize payment of medical benefits to the undersigned physician or supplier for services described below.

SIGNED _____

14. DATE OF CURRENT: MM   DD   YY   ILLNESS (First symptom) OR INJURY (Accident) OR PREGNANCY(LMP)

15. IF PATIENT HAS HAD SAME OR SIMILAR ILLNESS. GIVE FIRST DATE   MM   DD   YY

16. DATES PATIENT UNABLE TO WORK IN CURRENT OCCUPATION   MM   DD   YY   FROM   TO   MM   DD   YY

17. NAME OF REFERRING PHYSICIAN OR OTHER SOURCE

17a. I.D. NUMBER OF REFERRING PHYSICIAN

18. HOSPITALIZATION DATES RELATED TO CURRENT SERVICES   MM   DD   YY   FROM   TO   MM   DD   YY

19. RESERVED FOR LOCAL USE

20. OUTSIDE LAB?   YES   NO $ CHARGES

21. DIAGNOSIS OR NATURE OF ILLNESS OR INJURY. (RELATE ITEMS 1,2,3 OR 4 TO ITEM 24E BY LINE)

1. |___.___| 3. |___.___|

2. |___.___| 4. |___.___|

22. MEDICAID RESUBMISSION CODE   ORIGINAL REF. NO.

23. PRIOR AUTHORIZATION NUMBER

24. A						B	C	D		E	F	G	H	I	J	K
DATE(S) OF SERVICE						Place of Service	Type of Service	PROCEDURES, SERVICES, OR SUPPLIES (Explain Unusual Circumstances)		DIAGNOSIS CODE	$ CHARGES	DAYS OR UNITS	EPSDT Family Plan	EMG	COB	RESERVED FOR LOCAL USE
From			To					CPT/HCPCS	MODIFIER							
MM	DD	YY	MM	DD	YY											
1																
2																
3																
4																
5																
6																

25. FEDERAL TAX I.D. NUMBER   SSN   EIN

26. PATIENT'S ACCOUNT NO.

27. ACCEPT ASSIGNMENT? (For govt. claims, see back)   YES   NO

28. TOTAL CHARGE $

29. AMOUNT PAID $

30. BALANCE DUE $

31. SIGNATURE OF PHYSICIAN OR SUPPLIER INCLUDING DEGREES OR CREDENTIALS (I certify that the statements on the reverse apply to this bill and are made a part thereof.)

SIGNED _____   DATE _____

32. NAME AND ADDRESS OF FACILITY WHERE SERVICES WERE RENDERED (If other than home or office)

33. PHYSICIAN'S, SUPPLIER'S BILLING NAME, ADDRESS, ZIP CODE & PHONE #

PIN#   GRP#

(APPROVED BY AMA COUNCIL ON MEDICAL SERVICE 8/88)   **PLEASE PRINT OR TYPE**   APPROVED OMB-0938-0008 FORM CMS-1500 (12/90), FORM RRB-1500
APPROVED OMB-1215-0055 FORM OWCP-1500, APPROVED OMB-0720-0001 (CHAMPUS)

PLEASE
DO NOT
STAPLE
IN THIS
AREA

HEALTH INSURANCE CLAIM FORM

| | PICA | | | | | | | | PICA | |

1.
- [ ] MEDICARE (Medicare #)
- [ ] MEDICAID (Medicaid #)
- [ ] CHAMPUS (Sponsor's SSN)
- [ ] CHAMPVA (VA File #)
- [ ] GROUP HEALTH PLAN (SSN or ID)
- [ ] FECA BLK LUNG (SSN)
- [ ] OTHER (ID)

1a. INSURED'S I.D. NUMBER (FOR PROGRAM IN ITEM 1)

2. PATIENT'S NAME (Last Name, First Name, Middle Initial)

3. PATIENT'S BIRTH DATE MM | DD | YY   SEX M [ ] F [ ]

4. INSURED'S NAME (Last Name, First Name, Middle Initial)

5. PATIENT'S ADDRESS (No., Street)

6. PATIENT RELATIONSHIP TO INSURED
Self [ ] Spouse [ ] Child [ ] Other [ ]

7. INSURED'S ADDRESS (No., Street)

CITY   STATE

8. PATIENT STATUS
Single [ ] Married [ ] Other [ ]
Employed [ ] Full-Time Student [ ] Part-Time Student [ ]

CITY   STATE

ZIP CODE   TELEPHONE (Include Area Code) ( )

ZIP CODE   TELEPHONE (INCLUDE AREA CODE) ( )

9. OTHER INSURED'S NAME (Last Name, First Name, Middle Initial)

10. IS PATIENT'S CONDITION RELATED TO:

11. INSURED'S POLICY GROUP OR FECA NUMBER

a. OTHER INSURED'S POLICY OR GROUP NUMBER

a. EMPLOYMENT? (CURRENT OR PREVIOUS) YES [ ] NO [ ]

a. INSURED'S DATE OF BIRTH MM | DD | YY   SEX M [ ] F [ ]

b. OTHER INSURED'S DATE OF BIRTH MM | DD | YY   SEX M [ ] F [ ]

b. AUTO ACCIDENT?   PLACE (State) YES [ ] NO [ ]

b. EMPLOYER'S NAME OR SCHOOL NAME

c. EMPLOYER'S NAME OR SCHOOL NAME

c. OTHER ACCIDENT? YES [ ] NO [ ]

c. INSURANCE PLAN NAME OR PROGRAM NAME

d. INSURANCE PLAN NAME OR PROGRAM NAME

10d. RESERVED FOR LOCAL USE

d. IS THERE ANOTHER HEALTH BENEFIT PLAN?
YES [ ] NO [ ] If yes, return to and complete item 9 a-d.

READ BACK OF FORM BEFORE COMPLETING & SIGNING THIS FORM.

12. PATIENT'S OR AUTHORIZED PERSON'S SIGNATURE I authorize the release of any medical or other information necessary to process this claim. I also request payment of government benefits either to myself or to the party who accepts assignment below.

SIGNED   DATE

13. INSURED'S OR AUTHORIZED PERSON'S SIGNATURE I authorize payment of medical benefits to the undersigned physician or supplier for services described below.

SIGNED

14. DATE OF CURRENT: ILLNESS (First symptom) OR INJURY (Accident) OR PREGNANCY(LMP) MM | DD | YY

15. IF PATIENT HAS HAD SAME OR SIMILAR ILLNESS. GIVE FIRST DATE MM | DD | YY

16. DATES PATIENT UNABLE TO WORK IN CURRENT OCCUPATION MM | DD | YY FROM   TO MM | DD | YY

17. NAME OF REFERRING PHYSICIAN OR OTHER SOURCE

17a. I.D. NUMBER OF REFERRING PHYSICIAN

18. HOSPITALIZATION DATES RELATED TO CURRENT SERVICES MM | DD | YY FROM   TO MM | DD | YY

19. RESERVED FOR LOCAL USE

20. OUTSIDE LAB? YES [ ] NO [ ] $ CHARGES

21. DIAGNOSIS OR NATURE OF ILLNESS OR INJURY. (RELATE ITEMS 1,2,3 OR 4 TO ITEM 24E BY LINE)
1. L___ . ___
2. L___ . ___
3. L___ . ___
4. L___ . ___

22. MEDICAID RESUBMISSION CODE   ORIGINAL REF. NO.

23. PRIOR AUTHORIZATION NUMBER

24. A DATE(S) OF SERVICE From To MM DD YY MM DD YY	B Place of Service	C Type of Service	D PROCEDURES, SERVICES, OR SUPPLIES (Explain Unusual Circumstances) CPT/HCPCS	MODIFIER	E DIAGNOSIS CODE	F $ CHARGES	G DAYS OR UNITS	H EPSDT Family Plan	I EMG	J COB	K RESERVED FOR LOCAL USE
1											
2											
3											
4											
5											
6											

25. FEDERAL TAX I.D. NUMBER   SSN [ ] EIN [ ]

26. PATIENT'S ACCOUNT NO.

27. ACCEPT ASSIGNMENT? (For govt. claims, see back) YES [ ] NO [ ]

28. TOTAL CHARGE $

29. AMOUNT PAID $

30. BALANCE DUE $

31. SIGNATURE OF PHYSICIAN OR SUPPLIER INCLUDING DEGREES OR CREDENTIALS (I certify that the statements on the reverse apply to this bill and are made a part thereof.)

SIGNED   DATE

32. NAME AND ADDRESS OF FACILITY WHERE SERVICES WERE RENDERED (If other than home or office)

33. PHYSICIAN'S, SUPPLIER'S BILLING NAME, ADDRESS, ZIP CODE & PHONE #

PIN#   GRP#

(APPROVED BY AMA COUNCIL ON MEDICAL SERVICE 8/88)   **PLEASE PRINT OR TYPE**   APPROVED OMB-0938-0008 FORM CMS-1500 (12/90), FORM RRB-1500
APPROVED OMB-1215-0055 FORM OWCP-1500, APPROVED OMB-0720-0001 (CHAMPUS)

PLEASE
DO NOT
STAPLE
IN THIS
AREA

CARRIER

| | PICA | | | | | | | **HEALTH INSURANCE CLAIM FORM** | | PICA | |

1. MEDICARE MEDICAID CHAMPUS CHAMPVA GROUP HEALTH PLAN FECA BLK LUNG OTHER	1a. INSURED'S I.D. NUMBER	(FOR PROGRAM IN ITEM 1)
(Medicare #) (Medicaid #) (Sponsor's SSN) (VA File #) (SSN or ID) (SSN) (ID)		

2. PATIENT'S NAME (Last Name, First Name, Middle Initial)

3. PATIENT'S BIRTH DATE MM DD YY   SEX   M F

4. INSURED'S NAME (Last Name, First Name, Middle Initial)

5. PATIENT'S ADDRESS (No., Street)

6. PATIENT RELATIONSHIP TO INSURED   Self Spouse Child Other

7. INSURED'S ADDRESS (No., Street)

CITY   STATE

8. PATIENT STATUS   Single Married Other

CITY   STATE

ZIP CODE   TELEPHONE (Include Area Code) ( )

Employed Full-Time Student Part-Time Student

ZIP CODE   TELEPHONE (INCLUDE AREA CODE) ( )

9. OTHER INSURED'S NAME (Last Name, First Name, Middle Initial)

10. IS PATIENT'S CONDITION RELATED TO:

11. INSURED'S POLICY GROUP OR FECA NUMBER

a. OTHER INSURED'S POLICY OR GROUP NUMBER

a. EMPLOYMENT? (CURRENT OR PREVIOUS)   YES NO

a. INSURED'S DATE OF BIRTH MM DD YY   SEX   M F

b. OTHER INSURED'S DATE OF BIRTH MM DD YY   SEX   M F

b. AUTO ACCIDENT?   PLACE (State)   YES NO

b. EMPLOYER'S NAME OR SCHOOL NAME

c. EMPLOYER'S NAME OR SCHOOL NAME

c. OTHER ACCIDENT?   YES NO

c. INSURANCE PLAN NAME OR PROGRAM NAME

d. INSURANCE PLAN NAME OR PROGRAM NAME

10d. RESERVED FOR LOCAL USE

d. IS THERE ANOTHER HEALTH BENEFIT PLAN?   YES NO   *If yes*, return to and complete item 9 a-d.

READ BACK OF FORM BEFORE COMPLETING & SIGNING THIS FORM.

12. PATIENT'S OR AUTHORIZED PERSON'S SIGNATURE I authorize the release of any medical or other information necessary to process this claim. I also request payment of government benefits either to myself or to the party who accepts assignment below.

SIGNED _____ DATE _____

13. INSURED'S OR AUTHORIZED PERSON'S SIGNATURE I authorize payment of medical benefits to the undersigned physician or supplier for services described below.

SIGNED _____

14. DATE OF CURRENT: MM DD YY   ILLNESS (First symptom) OR INJURY (Accident) OR PREGNANCY(LMP)

15. IF PATIENT HAS HAD SAME OR SIMILAR ILLNESS. GIVE FIRST DATE MM DD YY

16. DATES PATIENT UNABLE TO WORK IN CURRENT OCCUPATION FROM MM DD YY TO MM DD YY

17. NAME OF REFERRING PHYSICIAN OR OTHER SOURCE

17a. I.D. NUMBER OF REFERRING PHYSICIAN

18. HOSPITALIZATION DATES RELATED TO CURRENT SERVICES FROM MM DD YY TO MM DD YY

19. RESERVED FOR LOCAL USE

20. OUTSIDE LAB?   YES NO $ CHARGES

21. DIAGNOSIS OR NATURE OF ILLNESS OR INJURY. (RELATE ITEMS 1,2,3 OR 4 TO ITEM 24E BY LINE)

1. |___.___   3. |___.___

2. |___.___   4. |___.___

22. MEDICAID RESUBMISSION CODE   ORIGINAL REF. NO.

23. PRIOR AUTHORIZATION NUMBER

24. A DATE(S) OF SERVICE						B Place of Service	C Type of Service	D PROCEDURES, SERVICES, OR SUPPLIES (Explain Unusual Circumstances) CPT/HCPCS MODIFIER	E DIAGNOSIS CODE	F $ CHARGES	G DAYS OR UNITS	H EPSDT Family Plan	I EMG	J COB	K RESERVED FOR LOCAL USE
From MM	DD	YY	To MM	DD	YY										
1															
2															
3															
4															
5															
6															

25. FEDERAL TAX I.D. NUMBER   SSN EIN

26. PATIENT'S ACCOUNT NO.

27. ACCEPT ASSIGNMENT? (For govt. claims, see back)   YES NO

28. TOTAL CHARGE $

29. AMOUNT PAID $

30. BALANCE DUE $

31. SIGNATURE OF PHYSICIAN OR SUPPLIER INCLUDING DEGREES OR CREDENTIALS (I certify that the statements on the reverse apply to this bill and are made a part thereof.)

SIGNED _____ DATE _____

32. NAME AND ADDRESS OF FACILITY WHERE SERVICES WERE RENDERED (If other than home or office)

33. PHYSICIAN'S, SUPPLIER'S BILLING NAME, ADDRESS, ZIP CODE & PHONE #

PIN#   GRP#

PATIENT AND INSURED INFORMATION

PHYSICIAN OR SUPPLIER INFORMATION

(APPROVED BY AMA COUNCIL ON MEDICAL SERVICE 8/88)   ***PLEASE PRINT OR TYPE***   APPROVED OMB-0938-0008 FORM CMS-1500 (12/90), FORM RRB-1500
APPROVED OMB-1215-0055 FORM OWCP-1500, APPROVED OMB-0720-0001 (CHAMPUS)

PLEASE
DO NOT
STAPLE
IN THIS
AREA

CARRIER

HEALTH INSURANCE CLAIM FORM

PICA ☐☐ | PICA ☐☐

1. MEDICARE ☐ (Medicare #) | MEDICAID ☐ (Medicaid #) | CHAMPUS ☐ (Sponsor's SSN) | CHAMPVA ☐ (VA File #) | GROUP HEALTH PLAN ☐ (SSN or ID) | FECA BLK LUNG ☐ (SSN) | OTHER ☐ (ID) | 1a. INSURED'S I.D. NUMBER (FOR PROGRAM IN ITEM 1)

2. PATIENT'S NAME (Last Name, First Name, Middle Initial) | 3. PATIENT'S BIRTH DATE MM | DD | YY SEX M ☐ F ☐ | 4. INSURED'S NAME (Last Name, First Name, Middle Initial)

5. PATIENT'S ADDRESS (No., Street) | 6. PATIENT RELATIONSHIP TO INSURED Self ☐ Spouse ☐ Child ☐ Other ☐ | 7. INSURED'S ADDRESS (No., Street)

CITY | STATE | 8. PATIENT STATUS Single ☐ Married ☐ Other ☐ | CITY | STATE

ZIP CODE | TELEPHONE (Include Area Code) ( ) | Employed ☐ Full-Time Student ☐ Part-Time Student ☐ | ZIP CODE | TELEPHONE (INCLUDE AREA CODE) ( )

9. OTHER INSURED'S NAME (Last Name, First Name, Middle Initial) | 10. IS PATIENT'S CONDITION RELATED TO: | 11. INSURED'S POLICY GROUP OR FECA NUMBER

a. OTHER INSURED'S POLICY OR GROUP NUMBER | a. EMPLOYMENT? (CURRENT OR PREVIOUS) YES ☐ NO ☐ | a INSURED'S DATE OF BIRTH MM | DD | YY SEX M ☐ F ☐

b. OTHER INSURED'S DATE OF BIRTH MM | DD | YY SEX M ☐ F ☐ | b. AUTO ACCIDENT? YES ☐ NO ☐ PLACE (State) | b. EMPLOYER'S NAME OR SCHOOL NAME

c. EMPLOYER'S NAME OR SCHOOL NAME | c. OTHER ACCIDENT? YES ☐ NO ☐ | c. INSURANCE PLAN NAME OR PROGRAM NAME

d. INSURANCE PLAN NAME OR PROGRAM NAME | 10d. RESERVED FOR LOCAL USE | d. IS THERE ANOTHER HEALTH BENEFIT PLAN? YES ☐ NO ☐ *If yes*, return to and complete item 9 a-d.

READ BACK OF FORM BEFORE COMPLETING & SIGNING THIS FORM.
12. PATIENT'S OR AUTHORIZED PERSON'S SIGNATURE I authorize the release of any medical or other information necessary to process this claim. I also request payment of government benefits either to myself or to the party who accepts assignment below.

SIGNED _____ DATE _____

13. INSURED'S OR AUTHORIZED PERSON'S SIGNATURE I authorize payment of medical benefits to the undersigned physician or supplier for services described below.

SIGNED _____

14. DATE OF CURRENT: ILLNESS (First symptom) OR INJURY (Accident) OR PREGNANCY(LMP) MM | DD | YY | 15. IF PATIENT HAS HAD SAME OR SIMILAR ILLNESS. GIVE FIRST DATE MM | DD | YY | 16. DATES PATIENT UNABLE TO WORK IN CURRENT OCCUPATION FROM MM | DD | YY TO MM | DD | YY

17. NAME OF REFERRING PHYSICIAN OR OTHER SOURCE | 17a. I.D. NUMBER OF REFERRING PHYSICIAN | 18. HOSPITALIZATION DATES RELATED TO CURRENT SERVICES FROM MM | DD | YY TO MM | DD | YY

19. RESERVED FOR LOCAL USE | 20. OUTSIDE LAB? YES ☐ NO ☐ $ CHARGES

21. DIAGNOSIS OR NATURE OF ILLNESS OR INJURY. (RELATE ITEMS 1,2,3 OR 4 TO ITEM 24E BY LINE)
1. |___.__ 3. |___.__
2. |___.__ 4. |___.__

22. MEDICAID RESUBMISSION CODE | ORIGINAL REF. NO.

23. PRIOR AUTHORIZATION NUMBER

24. A DATE(S) OF SERVICE From MM DD YY To MM DD YY	B Place of Service	C Type of Service	D PROCEDURES, SERVICES, OR SUPPLIES (Explain Unusual Circumstances) CPT/HCPCS | MODIFIER	E DIAGNOSIS CODE	F $ CHARGES	G DAYS OR UNITS	H EPSDT Family Plan	I EMG	J COB	K RESERVED FOR LOCAL USE
1										
2										
3										
4										
5										
6										

25. FEDERAL TAX I.D. NUMBER SSN ☐ EIN ☐ | 26. PATIENT'S ACCOUNT NO. | 27. ACCEPT ASSIGNMENT? (For govt. claims, see back) YES ☐ NO ☐ | 28. TOTAL CHARGE $ | 29. AMOUNT PAID $ | 30. BALANCE DUE $

31. SIGNATURE OF PHYSICIAN OR SUPPLIER INCLUDING DEGREES OR CREDENTIALS (I certify that the statements on the reverse apply to this bill and are made a part thereof.)

SIGNED _____ DATE _____

32. NAME AND ADDRESS OF FACILITY WHERE SERVICES WERE RENDERED (If other than home or office)

33. PHYSICIAN'S, SUPPLIER'S BILLING NAME, ADDRESS, ZIP CODE & PHONE #

PIN# _____ GRP# _____

(APPROVED BY AMA COUNCIL ON MEDICAL SERVICE 8/88) **PLEASE PRINT OR TYPE**

APPROVED OMB-0938-0008 FORM CMS-1500 (12/90), FORM RRB-1500
APPROVED OMB-1215-0055 FORM OWCP-1500, APPROVED OMB-0720-0001 (CHAMPUS)

PATIENT AND INSURED INFORMATION

PHYSICIAN OR SUPPLIER INFORMATION

PLEASE
DO NOT
STAPLE
IN THIS
AREA

CARRIER →

HEALTH INSURANCE CLAIM FORM

PICA

| PICA | | |

| 1. MEDICARE | MEDICAID | CHAMPUS | CHAMPVA | GROUP HEALTH PLAN | FECA BLK LUNG | OTHER | 1a. INSURED'S I.D. NUMBER | (FOR PROGRAM IN ITEM 1) |

(Medicare #)   (Medicaid #)   (Sponsor's SSN)   (VA File #)   (SSN or ID)   (SSN)   (ID)

2. PATIENT'S NAME (Last Name, First Name, Middle Initial)

3. PATIENT'S BIRTH DATE   MM | DD | YY   SEX   M ☐   F ☐

4. INSURED'S NAME (Last Name, First Name, Middle Initial)

5. PATIENT'S ADDRESS (No., Street)

6. PATIENT RELATIONSHIP TO INSURED   Self ☐   Spouse ☐   Child ☐   Other ☐

7. INSURED'S ADDRESS (No., Street)

CITY   STATE

8. PATIENT STATUS   Single ☐   Married ☐   Other ☐

CITY   STATE

ZIP CODE   TELEPHONE (Include Area Code)   ( )

Employed ☐   Full-Time Student ☐   Part-Time Student ☐

ZIP CODE   TELEPHONE (INCLUDE AREA CODE)   ( )

9. OTHER INSURED'S NAME (Last Name, First Name, Middle Initial)

10. IS PATIENT'S CONDITION RELATED TO:

11. INSURED'S POLICY GROUP OR FECA NUMBER

a. OTHER INSURED'S POLICY OR GROUP NUMBER

a. EMPLOYMENT? (CURRENT OR PREVIOUS)   ☐ YES   ☐ NO

a. INSURED'S DATE OF BIRTH   MM | DD | YY   SEX   M ☐   F ☐

b. OTHER INSURED'S DATE OF BIRTH   MM | DD | YY   SEX   M ☐   F ☐

b. AUTO ACCIDENT?   PLACE (State)   ☐ YES   ☐ NO

b. EMPLOYER'S NAME OR SCHOOL NAME

c. EMPLOYER'S NAME OR SCHOOL NAME

c. OTHER ACCIDENT?   ☐ YES   ☐ NO

c. INSURANCE PLAN NAME OR PROGRAM NAME

d. INSURANCE PLAN NAME OR PROGRAM NAME

10d. RESERVED FOR LOCAL USE

d. IS THERE ANOTHER HEALTH BENEFIT PLAN?   ☐ YES   ☐ NO   *If yes*, return to and complete item 9 a-d.

READ BACK OF FORM BEFORE COMPLETING & SIGNING THIS FORM.

12. PATIENT'S OR AUTHORIZED PERSON'S SIGNATURE I authorize the release of any medical or other information necessary to process this claim. I also request payment of government benefits either to myself or to the party who accepts assignment below.

SIGNED _____ DATE _____

13. INSURED'S OR AUTHORIZED PERSON'S SIGNATURE I authorize payment of medical benefits to the undersigned physician or supplier for services described below.

SIGNED _____

14. DATE OF CURRENT: MM | DD | YY   ◄ ILLNESS (First symptom) OR INJURY (Accident) OR PREGNANCY(LMP)

15. IF PATIENT HAS HAD SAME OR SIMILAR ILLNESS. GIVE FIRST DATE   MM | DD | YY

16. DATES PATIENT UNABLE TO WORK IN CURRENT OCCUPATION   FROM MM | DD | YY   TO MM | DD | YY

17. NAME OF REFERRING PHYSICIAN OR OTHER SOURCE

17a. I.D. NUMBER OF REFERRING PHYSICIAN

18. HOSPITALIZATION DATES RELATED TO CURRENT SERVICES   FROM MM | DD | YY   TO MM | DD | YY

19. RESERVED FOR LOCAL USE

20. OUTSIDE LAB?   ☐ YES   ☐ NO $ CHARGES

21. DIAGNOSIS OR NATURE OF ILLNESS OR INJURY. (RELATE ITEMS 1,2,3 OR 4 TO ITEM 24E BY LINE)

1. L___.___   3. L___.___
2. L___.___   4. L___.___

22. MEDICAID RESUBMISSION CODE   ORIGINAL REF. NO.

23. PRIOR AUTHORIZATION NUMBER

| 24. | A DATE(S) OF SERVICE | | | | | | B Place of Service | C Type of Service | D PROCEDURES, SERVICES, OR SUPPLIES (Explain Unusual Circumstances) CPT/HCPCS \| MODIFIER | E DIAGNOSIS CODE | F $ CHARGES | G DAYS OR UNITS | H EPSDT Family Plan | I EMG | J COB | K RESERVED FOR LOCAL USE |
	From MM	DD	YY	To MM	DD	YY										
1																
2																
3																
4																
5																
6																

25. FEDERAL TAX I.D. NUMBER   SSN ☐ EIN ☐

26. PATIENT'S ACCOUNT NO.

27. ACCEPT ASSIGNMENT? (For govt. claims, see back)   ☐ YES   ☐ NO

28. TOTAL CHARGE $

29. AMOUNT PAID $

30. BALANCE DUE $

31. SIGNATURE OF PHYSICIAN OR SUPPLIER INCLUDING DEGREES OR CREDENTIALS (I certify that the statements on the reverse apply to this bill and are made a part thereof.)

SIGNED _____ DATE _____

32. NAME AND ADDRESS OF FACILITY WHERE SERVICES WERE RENDERED (If other than home or office)

33. PHYSICIAN'S, SUPPLIER'S BILLING NAME, ADDRESS, ZIP CODE & PHONE #

PIN#   GRP#

(APPROVED BY AMA COUNCIL ON MEDICAL SERVICE 8/88)   **PLEASE PRINT OR TYPE**   APPROVED OMB-0938-0008 FORM CMS-1500 (12/90), FORM RRB-1500
APPROVED OMB-1215-0055 FORM OWCP-1500, APPROVED OMB-0720-0001 (CHAMPUS)

PATIENT AND INSURED INFORMATION   PHYSICIAN OR SUPPLIER INFORMATION

CARRIER

PLEASE
DO NOT
STAPLE
IN THIS
AREA

| | PICA | | | | | | | | | | |

HEALTH INSURANCE CLAIM FORM

PICA

1. MEDICARE	MEDICAID	CHAMPUS	CHAMPVA	GROUP HEALTH PLAN	FECA BLK LUNG	OTHER	1a. INSURED'S I.D. NUMBER	(FOR PROGRAM IN ITEM 1)
(Medicare #)	(Medicaid #)	(Sponsor's SSN)	(VA File #)	(SSN or ID)	(SSN)	(ID)		

2. PATIENT'S NAME (Last Name, First Name, Middle Initial)

3. PATIENT'S BIRTH DATE
MM   DD   YY   SEX
M   F

4. INSURED'S NAME (Last Name, First Name, Middle Initial)

5. PATIENT'S ADDRESS (No., Street)

6. PATIENT RELATIONSHIP TO INSURED
Self   Spouse   Child   Other

7. INSURED'S ADDRESS (No., Street)

CITY   STATE

8. PATIENT STATUS
Single   Married   Other
Employed   Full-Time Student   Part-Time Student

CITY   STATE

ZIP CODE   TELEPHONE (Include Area Code)
( )

ZIP CODE   TELEPHONE (INCLUDE AREA CODE)
( )

9. OTHER INSURED'S NAME (Last Name, First Name, Middle Initial)

10. IS PATIENT'S CONDITION RELATED TO:

11. INSURED'S POLICY GROUP OR FECA NUMBER

a. OTHER INSURED'S POLICY OR GROUP NUMBER

a. EMPLOYMENT? (CURRENT OR PREVIOUS)
YES   NO

a. INSURED'S DATE OF BIRTH
MM   DD   YY   SEX
M   F

b. OTHER INSURED'S DATE OF BIRTH
MM   DD   YY   SEX
M   F

b. AUTO ACCIDENT?   PLACE (State)
YES   NO

b. EMPLOYER'S NAME OR SCHOOL NAME

c. EMPLOYER'S NAME OR SCHOOL NAME

c. OTHER ACCIDENT?
YES   NO

c. INSURANCE PLAN NAME OR PROGRAM NAME

d. INSURANCE PLAN NAME OR PROGRAM NAME

10d. RESERVED FOR LOCAL USE

d. IS THERE ANOTHER HEALTH BENEFIT PLAN?
YES   NO   If yes, return to and complete item 9 a-d.

READ BACK OF FORM BEFORE COMPLETING & SIGNING THIS FORM.
12. PATIENT'S OR AUTHORIZED PERSON'S SIGNATURE I authorize the release of any medical or other information necessary to process this claim. I also request payment of government benefits either to myself or to the party who accepts assignment below.

SIGNED _____ DATE _____

13. INSURED'S OR AUTHORIZED PERSON'S SIGNATURE I authorize payment of medical benefits to the undersigned physician or supplier for services described below.

SIGNED _____

PATIENT AND INSURED INFORMATION

14. DATE OF CURRENT: ILLNESS (First symptom) OR
MM   DD   YY   INJURY (Accident) OR
                       PREGNANCY(LMP)

15. IF PATIENT HAS HAD SAME OR SIMILAR ILLNESS. GIVE FIRST DATE   MM   DD   YY

16. DATES PATIENT UNABLE TO WORK IN CURRENT OCCUPATION
MM   DD   YY   MM   DD   YY
FROM   TO

17. NAME OF REFERRING PHYSICIAN OR OTHER SOURCE

17a. I.D. NUMBER OF REFERRING PHYSICIAN

18. HOSPITALIZATION DATES RELATED TO CURRENT SERVICES
MM   DD   YY   MM   DD   YY
FROM   TO

19. RESERVED FOR LOCAL USE

20. OUTSIDE LAB? $ CHARGES
YES   NO

21. DIAGNOSIS OR NATURE OF ILLNESS OR INJURY. (RELATE ITEMS 1,2,3 OR 4 TO ITEM 24E BY LINE)

1. |___.___| 3. |___.___|

2. |___.___| 4. |___.___|

22. MEDICAID RESUBMISSION
CODE   ORIGINAL REF. NO.

23. PRIOR AUTHORIZATION NUMBER

24. A DATE(S) OF SERVICE						B Place of Service	C Type of Service	D PROCEDURES, SERVICES, OR SUPPLIES (Explain Unusual Circumstances) CPT/HCPCS MODIFIER	E DIAGNOSIS CODE	F $ CHARGES	G DAYS OR UNITS	H EPSDT Family Plan	I EMG	J COB	K RESERVED FOR LOCAL USE
From MM	DD	YY	To MM	DD	YY										
1															
2															
3															
4															
5															
6															

25. FEDERAL TAX I.D. NUMBER   SSN EIN

26. PATIENT'S ACCOUNT NO.

27. ACCEPT ASSIGNMENT?
(For govt. claims, see back)
YES   NO

28. TOTAL CHARGE
$

29. AMOUNT PAID
$

30. BALANCE DUE
$

31. SIGNATURE OF PHYSICIAN OR SUPPLIER INCLUDING DEGREES OR CREDENTIALS
(I certify that the statements on the reverse apply to this bill and are made a part thereof.)

SIGNED _____ DATE _____

32. NAME AND ADDRESS OF FACILITY WHERE SERVICES WERE RENDERED (If other than home or office)

33. PHYSICIAN'S, SUPPLIER'S BILLING NAME, ADDRESS, ZIP CODE & PHONE #

PIN#   GRP#

PHYSICIAN OR SUPPLIER INFORMATION

(APPROVED BY AMA COUNCIL ON MEDICAL SERVICE 8/88)   **PLEASE PRINT OR TYPE**

APPROVED OMB-0938-0008 FORM CMS-1500 (12/90), FORM RRB-1500
APPROVED OMB-1215-0055 FORM OWCP-1500, APPROVED OMB-0720-0001 (CHAMPUS)